William Grant

Elizabeth Gage
A Life in Jewellery

ACC ART BOOKS

Contents

Introduction

In 1963, an attractive young art student enrolled at the Sir John Cass College in London to study silversmithing. A year later, she transferred to the jewellery department under the tutelage of Frank Oliver. Her name was Elizabeth Gage; and, at the time, she was the only woman in a class of 30.

Despite coming from a wealthy Anglo-American family, Elizabeth had a childhood that was far from idyllic. A protracted illness meant that much of her time was spent under the care of various doctors and nurses in London and, later, in New York, where her parents desperately sought a cure. Bedridden for extended periods, she amused herself by drawing pictures and making clothes and houses for her dolls.

That this fledgling display of artistic proclivity and manual dexterity proved to be formative was unsurprising: both her mother and maternal grandmother were accomplished artists whose works had been exhibited in prestigious galleries on both sides of the Atlantic.

Elizabeth Gage's motivation for learning the craft of making jewellery had its origins in an idle moment wandering through the British Museum. Her boyfriend at the time had promised to buy her a ring as a present but she had been unable to find anything she liked in the shops. She wasn't fond of the Victorian and Edwardian styles that still influenced the jewellery scene at the time; they seemed outdated and somewhat fussy to her. Nor was she much interested in emulating the recently arrived modernist movement, with its sharp angles and abstracted forms. Now suddenly, in a cabinet in front of her, was a display of ancient, hammered gold rings that spoke to her soul.

A momentary impulse to smash and grab was readily suppressed and replaced with the notion that, in order to possess such objects of desire, she might actually have to make them herself. Thus began a 60-year (and counting) career that no other British-born woman has come close to matching – let alone eclipsing – in terms of enduring commercial success, strength of design and international renown.

Acknowledgement of Elizabeth Gage's talent as a designer came early with a commission from Cartier in 1968. This was followed, in 1972, by a coveted De Beers Diamonds International Award; the 'Oscar' of the jewellery world. The business flourished and by 1989, Elizabeth's burgeoning contribution to the nation's economic output was recognised with The Queen's Award for Export Achievement. Her most recent and cherished accolade came in 2017, when she was named in the Queen's Birthday Honours List to receive an MBE, which was presented to her at Buckingham Palace.

Elizabeth Gage has managed to achieve these notable accomplishments without ever compromising on standards, craftsmanship or creative integrity. Every piece of jewellery that bears her name is the product of her artistic virtuosity and is still handmade in England by goldsmiths, enamellers and gem setters who have mastered their craft and the art of making Elizabeth Gage jewellery.

Her bold, colourful designs inspired by nature and history, as well as her unique expression of unconventional creativity, are so instantly recognisable that whenever clients encounter one another at social gatherings there is an inevitable reflex nod of mutual acknowledgement and approbation, as if to say: 'I don't believe we've met but I admire your style' and this, as much as anything else, represents the ultimate seal of approval.

Elizabeth Gage at her workbench, circa 1969
[© Elizabeth Gage]

CHAPTER 1
Childhood

Previous page: Elizabeth Gage, New York, in 1941. [© Elizabeth Gage]

Left: Thalia Wescott Millett, circa 1930. [© Elizabeth Gage]

Right: Edward Gage photographed with his English Bull Terrier, circa 1930. [© Elizabeth Gage]

Elizabeth Estling Gage was born at home in London on 31 December 1937 in Brook Street, Mayfair. The youngest of three, her elder siblings are Anne (b. 25 November 1931) and Robert, known as 'Robin' (b. 19 April 1934). Elizabeth's American mother, Thalia, and English father, Edward, were married in London on 21 January 1931.

Thalia Gage (née Westcott Millett, b.1906) was an accomplished poet and artist. Her paintings were exhibited internationally, including at the Redfern and Mayor galleries in London, Midtown Galleries in New York, George Washington University in Washington, D.C., Galerie André Weil and the Salon d'Automne in Paris, and the Musée Ingres in Montauban. In addition to painting, Thalia was awarded numerous prizes for poetry (composed in French) by, amongst others, La Société des Poètes et Artistes de France. Thalia inherited her artistic ability from her mother, also named Thalia, who painted under her married surname 'Malcolm' (from her second husband) and was known in the family as 'Granny Malcolm'.

Elizabeth's father, Edward Fitzhardinge Peyton Gage, also born in 1906, was the great-grandson of Henry Hall, 4th Viscount Gage of Castle Island. By tradition, the family is believed to have descended from a Norman baron Sire de Gaugi, who accompanied William the Conqueror in 1066 and fought at the Battle of Hastings. The family name was later anglicised to Gage. Edward Gage duly embarked on the conventional trajectory of an English gentleman: namely Eton, Oxford, the Coldstream Guards and a career in the City.

The lake view of Rake Manor, Surrey. [© Elizabeth Gage]

The garden view of Rake Manor, Surrey. [© Elizabeth Gage]

Thalia Westcott Malcolm ('Granny Malcolm') at her easel, circa late 1940s. [© Elizabeth Gage]

The Gage family lived in London during the week (at 67 Brook Street, where Elizabeth was born), and at Rake Manor, a timber-framed Elizabethan property near Godalming, Surrey for weekends and holidays. Rake had been gifted to Elizabeth's parents in 1931 as a wedding present from Granny Malcolm.

At the outbreak of the Second World War, Elizabeth's father's battalion was part of the British Expeditionary Force, which fought in the Battle of France. He was subsequently evacuated from Dunkirk back to England in 1940. His next campaign was with the Guards Armoured Division fighting German and Italian forces in North Africa.

The family would sometimes holiday at Malbosquet in Vence, a grand villa set in the hills above Nice on the Côte d'Azur, owned by Elizabeth's maternal grandmother, Granny Malcolm. In the summer of 1939, *en route* to Malbosquet, Elizabeth contracted bovine tuberculosis from drinking unpasteurised cow's milk that hadn't been heated properly. Initially, she was hospitalised in London but the treatment she received proved ineffective. Her mother was advised by the doctors that an alternative cure was available in America and that, if possible, Elizabeth should be sent to New York. There she could stay with Granny Malcolm and be placed under the care of American doctors. Soon after, Elizabeth was on a boat to New York accompanied by a nurse.

Malbosquet, Vence, South of France. [© Elizabeth Gage]

The garden at Malbosquet, Vence, South of France. [© Elizabeth Gage]

'I have no memory of the nurse or my voyage until we passed the Statue of Liberty. We disembarked and were taken to a large waiting area. The room was filled with trestle tables labelled A to Z...our luggage arrived at table G. My grandmother was there, and she welcomed me. I think I remembered her from France, but I was not sure about anything. We got in a car and arrived at Granny's Manhattan apartment on East 72nd Street.'

Elizabeth's siblings, Anne and Robin, had already gone with their grandmother to be schooled in America. Her mother, however, was obliged to remain in England at this time as 80 French cadets were due to be billeted at Rake Manor prior to undergoing training for the Free French Forces under General Charles de Gaulle. She received a warmly worded letter signed by the General thanking her for taking care of his 'young trainees' but later discovered that, sadly, only two of them had managed to survive the war.

Elizabeth's time in America was marked by bouts of illness followed by periods of remission. She was placed under the supervision of the inauspiciously named Doctor Coffin and a Nurse Roberts, whom she did not particularly like.

'I vividly remember Nurse Roberts telling me she was going out to dinner, but I was not to ask for a potty while she was away. Of course, I needed one and called for someone to bring it. Next day, Nurse Roberts came to see me, and she spanked me for doing what I had needed to do.'

Being ill meant that much of Elizabeth's early life was spent in bed on her doctor's orders. As a consequence, she fell into the habit of reading and started to make things with her hands – dolls' clothes, cardboard cut-out doll's houses and boxes – to keep herself occupied.

'The houses were my favourite because my imagination took me inside them and I thought about and visualised coloured silks from Arabia, carpets from Istanbul and the wonderful pictures painted by my grandmother hanging in my bedroom. The manual dexterity this developed stayed with me like a faithful dog.'

By the late summer of 1941, Elizabeth began to suffer from abdominal pains caused by a blocked intestine. Upon hearing that Elizabeth would require surgery, Thalia tried to arrange passage to New York to be with her daughter, but the Foreign Office said they were very sorry, but they could do nothing for her.

Undeterred, she recalled a chance encounter in Paris at the outset of the war and acted on the tried and tested maxim of well-connected people: 'If you want something done…go to the top!' The gentleman she called for assistance was an American, John Gilbert Winant. Thalia had started chatting to him at Orly airport as they were both waiting in a long queue for tickets to London.

'After an hour or so, he told Mummy he was going back to the Hôtel de Crillon in Place de la Concorde. Off he went. My mother, when she had her ticket, went to the Crillon to tell him she had heard there was another plane coming. He was so thankful of what she said. He told her that he was going to be the US Ambassador to London and that if ever she needed help, she should call him.'

Thalia telephoned the American Embassy and asked to speak with The Ambassador. The following day the phone rang; it was the Foreign Office: 'I see you have friends in high places. If we can't help you, Ambassador Winant would be very upset'. Thalia duly caught a plane to New York and arrived in time for the operation.

Elizabeth's father followed soon after. Having fought with distinction in France and North Africa, Major Gage, by then 35 years old, was granted compassionate leave to visit his daughter in New York and, subsequently, accepted a diplomatic position at the British Embassy in Washington, D.C. – a not altogether unfamiliar posting as his father had been military attaché there before the First World War.

'One day, a handsome man, dressed in his uniform came to see me. In a broad American accent, I said: "Are you my daddy? Will you read me Peter Rabbit?"'

While he was in New York, the nurse asked to have a meeting with Elizabeth's father to discuss her future.

'Nurse Roberts came to see Daddy. She said to my father that she wished to adopt me as I would never live a proper life. My Father replied: "If that is so, then she is coming home with me." I remember to this day that I arrived at the station in Washington dressed in a white blouse and a tartan skirt. With my father, was a lady called Thorby (my new nanny), whom I soon came to love. I remember her taking me in my pushchair down Broad Branch Road in Washington, D.C. Thorby was my treasure for many years and was with me when I came home to Rake Manor in Surrey.'

The Gage family remained in Washington, D.C. until after the Allied victory in Europe had been declared in the spring of 1945, when they took a boat back to England.

'The trip to go to England was my first experience of fear. We were sailing without life jackets, and I remember clutching my Hershey [chocolate] bars to my tummy. I knew we were in dangerous waters and that even though Germany had surrendered, Japan had not, and apparently there were Japanese submarines around. We came through alright and soon we were speeding in the car to Rake.'

Life in Surrey was all very new to Elizabeth, but she was happy to be with her family and to be cared for by Nanny Thorby. She enjoyed sailing on the lake in her new blow-up dinghy from Hamleys and watching the big pike splashing about.

Still too frail to go to school, Elizabeth was educated by a governess at home until, at the age of 12, her parents sent her to board at Westonbirt, an independent girls' school in Gloucestershire. Elizabeth admits to never being a great scholar but remembers enjoying Art and French. When asked about exams, her stock response is: 'The less said the better!'

In 1949, while Elizabeth was in her first year at Westonbirt, her parents sold Rake Manor after her father inherited Chyknell Hall Estate in Shropshire, from a cousin. He later acquired another property, Château de Combecave, in southern France, which, in time, became the main family home. Edward and Thalia Gage would reside there for the rest of their lives; Thalia died there in June 1994 and Edward in May 2000. Elizabeth's exposure to France, its culture and its history, was to have a lifelong impact on her creative outlook.

Drawing by Elizabeth Gage, aged 4;
New York, in 1941. [© Elizabeth Gage]

Little Elizabeth
aged four

CHAPTER 2
Finding a Vocation

Previous page: Elizabeth Gage, London, 1964. [© Elizabeth Gage]

Left: Lion Ring (1964). Yellow gold with four lion heads. This piece was inspired by a visit to Benaki Museum in Athens. Private collection. [© Elizabeth Gage Ltd]

Opposite: Butterfly Pin (1964). Silver, lapis lazuli and turquoise. Private collection. [© Elizabeth Gage]

Elizabeth left Westonbirt when she was 16. At this time in her life, she did not have a consuming passion for painting or drawing but was good at both. So, for the want of something better to do, she decided to follow in her mother's and grandmother's footsteps and study art. Having enrolled at the Chelsea School of Art in 1956, she graduated in 1959; however, the experience had failed to light a fuse and there was no intention of pursuing fine art as a career. Elizabeth knew she had something in her but thus far had failed to navigate a path towards her eventual vocation.

The first time she encountered jewellery that genuinely excited her was in the early 1960s when she developed an interest in the story of Catherine the Great, Empress of Russia, and, in particular, her passion for collecting art and jewels.

'It made me aware of the intense beauty of jewellery.'

The Empress, who gained the crown by deposing her own husband, ruled Russia during the second half of the 18th century. Inspired by the ideas of the Enlightenment, she presided over a golden era that oversaw major advances in science and culture as well as the expansion of the Russian Empire. The Empress's jewellery collection was later sold off by the Bolsheviks at the end of the First World War and now resides in museums across the world, including some important diamond pieces at the V&A in London.

The second and most significant episode in Elizabeth's odyssey toward jewellery appreciation took place in a London museum. She had always been a voracious reader of history books, and it was whilst researching the enigmatic 18th-century mystic and alchemist The Count of St Germain, in the British Library, that she had her true 'epiphany'.

A boyfriend at the time had promised to buy her a ring as a present. Yet, despite having scoured half the jewellery boutiques in London, Elizabeth couldn't find anything she even remotely liked. One day at lunchtime she left the library, which at the time was contained within the British Museum and, on a whim, decided to wander up to the Viking room. All at once, the clouds parted, and a shaft of light pierced through a high window, falling onto a glass display cabinet containing an array of about 20 ancient rings, crafted in beaten yellow

gold. Here was the kind of ring Elizabeth liked. Reasoning that she was unlikely to be able to secure one of these particular specimens for herself, she determined to make her own. So, in that moment, she decided to train as a goldsmith… Though she still had to find answers to the questions of where and how.

In 1963, Elizabeth Gage attended the Sir John Cass College, initially hoping to enrol in the jewellery section. However, as this was still under construction, she joined the silver department instead.

'It was here that I made the butterfly pin, my first jewel. I took the design straight from a book. This taught me the art of cutting and forming metal. It was huge and quite impractical but still, I had the excitement of my first pin and imagined wearing it to my next party.'

Agincourt Ring (1972). Articulated, carved yellow gold set with brilliant-cut diamonds. This ring was awarded the De Beers Diamonds International Award in 1972. Private collection. [© Elizabeth Gage Ltd]

Opposite: Original Agincourt Ring (1967). Articulated yellow gold, brilliant-cut peridots and amethysts. Private collection. [© Elizabeth Gage Ltd]

In 1964, the College moved its growing School of Art into Central House in Aldgate, a modernist building opposite Whitechapel Art Gallery, and Elizabeth managed to persuade the jewellery tutor, Frank Oliver, to accept her on his course, which covered gold work, enamelling and stone setting. At the time she was the only woman in a class of 30.

'My teacher, Mr Oliver, took me through the rudiments of diamond mounting and as soon as I could, I asked to make a pin in gold. With my first sheet of gold, I started work. The pin was sold and is now lost in the mists of time.'

Elizabeth managed to sell most of the jewels she made at college but always to the same handful of customers; many people she encountered were too conservative for her bold designs. To begin with she concentrated on rings but soon added other types of jewellery to her repertoire. Some of her early pieces were influenced by ancient Greek jewels and by artefacts she had acquired in Crete. These included a collection of Minoan soapstone seals, which she incorporated into a pair of earrings and a pin (now in the possession of the V&A, London) in 1967. The island became not just a source of inspiration but also the place where she acquired new skills and techniques from a master goldsmith, whom she persuaded to take her on as an apprentice during the long summer holidays.

She often travelled to New York to visit her grandmother; and it was here, soon after graduating in 1968, that she was introduced by a friend to Cartier.

'I was fortunate because my first commission was for Cartier, New York. They ordered about 30 pieces, and I decided to have them made for me as I could not cope with making them all myself.'

The experience bolstered her confidence enormously and suddenly, aged 31, she knew exactly what she wanted to do with her life and was well on her way to establishing a successful career in jewellery.

1. Giant knot ring. 18K gold $165.
2. Lion claw chain. 18K gold. $800.
3. Lion head pendant. 18K gold. $525.
4. Letter opener. Sterling silver. $12.
5. Giant dome ring. Lapis and 18K gold. Can be worn on middle or index finger. $875.
6. St. George medallion. 18K gold and turquoise. $625. With lapis or coral, $590.

Advertisement for Elizabeth's Cartier collection. New York, 1968. [© Elizabeth Gage Ltd]

Opposite: Elizabeth Gage wears her Minoan Seal Pin. Yellow gold set with South Sea pearls and ancient steatite (soapstone) intaglios from the Greek island of Crete, 1967. [© Elizabeth Gage]

Her success was cemented when, in 1972 Elizabeth was the recipient of the prestigious De Beers Diamonds International Award for her Agincourt ring. Originally designed in 1967, the articulated gold ring set with peridots and amethysts, had been an instant classic; the 1972 award-winning version was set with brilliant-cut diamonds in deeply carved gold.

For almost half a century, the De Beers Diamonds International Awards discovered and celebrated brilliance in diamond jewellery design. Considered the 'Oscars' of the jewellery industry, they were the most coveted and prestigious awards for excellence in jewellery design and craftsmanship. Winning entries required designers to create exceptional jewels with strong narratives, meticulous detail and fine craftsmanship.

Having originated in 1953, the awards were the source of some of the most original and influential designs in diamond jewellery and jewellery in general. The last edition of these biennial competitions took place in 2000.

In 1972, the Awards committee hailed Elizabeth's Agincourt ring an engineering masterpiece. It was unusual for a woman at that time to win such a prestigious award in a male-dominated industry. And it was an important step in establishing Elizabeth Gage as one of a new group of designers who challenged traditional jewellery designs with her distinctive and creative pieces.

CHAPTER 3

Establishing the Business

By the early 1970s Elizabeth Gage was selling to a few independent retailers in London and America.

'They liked my unique designs for their clients, so I was lucky enough to be able to produce one-of-a-kind pieces at a very early stage in my career. I also had a small network of private clients.'

Her next step was to take a space in the basement of jewellery boutique Annabel Jones, in 52 Beauchamp Place, where she installed a workbench. The pieces Elizabeth made were sold in the shop above. Annabel Jones, the owner of the eponymously named boutique, later married William, 4th Viscount Astor in 1976. Lady Astor went on to co-found the highly successful home furnishing designs company OKA. Elizabeth Gage's commercial relationship with Annabel Jones lasted into the mid 1970s and was the venue for her first one-woman show in 1972.

Located in Knightsbridge, and a stone's throw from Harrods, Beauchamp Place was home to numerous fashionable boutiques as well as San Lorenzo, the Italian restaurant and celebrity hang-out favoured by Diana, Princess of Wales, Jack Nicholson and Eric Clapton, among others. It was the perfect location from which to solicit the custom of London's smart set.

Elizabeth continued to cultivate her nascent jewellery business on both sides of the Atlantic and soon enough demand was growing at such a rate that she could not keep up making the jewellery just by herself. She subsequently decided to employ other goldsmiths and to focus instead on designing.

'Much as I loved making, I had to choose between this and designing. I chose the latter path. I still made occasionally when I had the time, and my training was a huge help to me.'

In 1973, she participated in the V&A's Craft exhibition and, that same year, was commissioned by Yale University to design and make a presentation piece for John Hay Whitney, former US Ambassador to the United Kingdom, proprietor of the *New York Herald Tribune* and President of the Museum of Modern Art. Elizabeth's profile in the US was further enhanced by an exhibition at the British Embassy, Washington in 1976 and her participation in the Virginia Craftsmen exhibition at The Richmond Museum, Virginia in 1977.

By the late 1970s, Elizabeth concluded that the business was sufficiently well established to invest in her own premises. She already knew her preference with regards to location, and when a place became available at the Garden House in Beauchamp Place, she took over the lease and opened her first shop in 1979. She enlisted the help of her Aunt Lillian, wife of her father's elder brother, Sir Berkeley Gage, who came to work with her. Elizabeth took on the selling role in the shop while her aunt ran the office upstairs.

Previous page: Elizabeth Gage with Budda at 20 Albemarle Street, London, 1984. [© Elizabeth Gage]

Opposite: Annabel Jones, circa 1975. [© Phillip Jackson/Daily Mail/Shutterstock]

20 Albemarle Street, Mayfair, London, in 1984. [© Elizabeth Gage]

Opposite: Inside 20 Albemarle Street, Mayfair, London, in 1984.
[© Elizabeth Gage]

The loss of his wife at home was initially a gross inconvenience to Sir Berkeley and there was a degree of tittering when he habitually phoned to announce that the lights had gone out or that there was no hot water...only to be told to work it out for himself!

The shop in Beauchamp Place helped to grow sales at a healthy rate until 1984, when Elizabeth decided to scale up once again by taking the lease on a showroom at 20 Albemarle Street. Opening such a large space in the heart of Mayfair was a considerable financial undertaking requiring Elizabeth to sell her house in France to cover the cost of the lease and the shopfitting.

'It was a huge jump but absolutely what was required, and this was the best way to expand.'

The previous leaseholder had also been a jeweller, so there were already a number of showcases set into the wall; to these were added freestanding showcases. The decorating scheme – incorporating antique French furniture, opulently printed fabrics and wallpaper, and redesigned packaging and display materials – was devised by Elizabeth with characteristically fanatical attention to detail. This colourful, ultra-feminine French 'salon' style became synonymous with Elizabeth Gage's personal aesthetic and presented a refreshing contrast to the more masculine décor of her competitors around the corner on Bond Street.

The move was well timed as an article on her work had recently appeared in *Connoisseur*, an American magazine covering luxury topics such as fine art, collectibles and antique furniture.

'Soon many American clients came flooding into the shop for the first time – waving the article! All the hard work that had taken place before the doors of my shop opened had suddenly paid off.'

Another fortuitous consequence of the move to 20 Albemarle Street was that Elizabeth got to meet and, soon after, employ Zoë Simpson; Zoë had shown her the property and helped negotiate the lease. It was the beginning of a 30-year working relationship that allowed Elizabeth to focus her attention on designing and selling in the knowledge that she had a capable and trusted lieutenant to take care of the administrative and operational aspects of what was by now a rapidly expanding business.

The opening of 20 Albemarle Street in the early 1980s coincided with the launch of a series of solo shows hosted by Elizabeth at various exclusive venues overseas, including the British Embassy and Hôtel Plaza Athénée in Paris; the Ritz-Carlton, Carlyle and Four Seasons hotels in New York; Beverly Wilshire and Bel-Air hotels in Los Angeles; The Ritz-Carlton hotels in Houston, San Francisco and Atlanta; Four Seasons and Drake hotels in Chicago; and the Mandarin Oriental in Hong Kong.

Over time, the exhibitions proved to be fundamental in growing Elizabeth's overseas customer base, though not all passed off without incident. On one occasion, in the autumn of 1988, the British Ambassador Sir Ewen Fergusson kindly offered to host a soirée at the British Embassy to launch Elizabeth's first Paris exhibition. Her moving crew delivered the showcases to the embassy and at the same time decanted a pair of palms into large silver plant pots that had apparently been left for the purpose. The following morning everything (including the silver planters) was moved back to the Hôtel Plaza Athénée for the main exhibition, with just a few complaints from the moving team, and hints about danger money, when they realised just how heavy they were.

After the exhibition suite at the Plaza Athénée had been dressed and finished and everything was perfectly arranged, the phone rang, and a rather panicked British Embassy official asked to speak to whoever was in charge. He went on to explain that a set of valuable solid silver jardinières had gone missing and unless they were returned within the hour, the gendarmerie would have to be alerted about the theft of these irreplaceable treasures!

Having initially assured him that only company-owned items had been removed from the embassy, Elizabeth looked around, saw the jardinières and realised to her horror what had occurred. She dispatched them back to the embassy post-haste along with a grovelling handwritten apology for the 'confusion'. The movers were perhaps the least amused as they had struggled with their immense weight the first time around!

On another occasion, returning from an exhibition in New York, Elizabeth had fallen asleep on the plane only to notice, on landing, that one of her large gold earrings was missing. A precursory search of the vicinity yielded nothing, so she asked the crew for assistance – again to no avail. Eventually an engineer was summoned to dismantle the seat but still there was no sign of the earring. Finally, about an hour after all the other passengers had left the aircraft, Elizabeth, for some unfathomable reason, decided to search her own person and located the missing, 'peanut shell' earring, which had fallen into her brassière. Perhaps it was relief, but everyone found the incident to be highly amusing; everyone, that is, except for the British Airways maintenance engineer!

Hotel exhibitions are often described as 'trunk shows' but as far as Elizabeth Gage was concerned, she insisted on having both the trunk *and* the elephant! A typical exhibition involved renting the largest double suite available for a week; installing eight freestanding showcases replete with jewels exclusively designed for the event; an armed security detail; a print advertising campaign; and invitations handwritten in calligraphy.

Meticulous planning, exclusive product and opulent surroundings were not the only elements necessary to ensure a successful exhibition, however. Elizabeth is naturally gregarious and a consummate hostess. She has a charming and friendly disposition towards anyone she encounters, no matter their social standing. As such, dealing with clients is for her a delight rather than a chore, and it is not surprising that many have become close friends.

Elizabeth Gage and the British Ambassador Sir Ewen Fergusson with Lady Fergusson at a reception given in honour of Elizabeth Gage on 21 November 1988 at the British Embassy in Paris. [Courtesy of Elizabeth Gage]

On behalf of HM Queen Elizabeth II, Lord Bramall presents Elizabeth Gage with the Queen's Award for Export Achievement in 1989. [Courtesy of Elizabeth Gage]

Opposite: Leopard jasper and onyx pendant necklace with 19th-century carnelian intaglio and quilted gold detailing, photographed with matching earrings. The necklace was acquired by Jacqueline Kennedy Onassis in 1991. [© Elizabeth Gage Ltd]

The business of entertaining and socialising, therefore, became a critical adjunct to the main event, beginning with an opening night cocktail party and followed by endless rounds of dinners and lunches with staff and clients. Despite being exhausting, and potentially ruinously expensive, the exhibitions proved to be an immediate commercial success.

Perhaps the most notable encounter of these solo shows in the United States occurred in New York. One morning, a lady telephoned enquiring about a necklace she had seen advertised in a magazine and asked if she could view it. An appointment was arranged and later that day a noticeably stylish and elegant woman arrived at the hotel suite and duly purchased the necklace. The lady in question was Jacqueline Kennedy Onassis.

Elizabeth's overseas exhibitions served to accelerate sales abroad, particularly in the US, to the extent that, in 1989, Elizabeth Gage was awarded the prestigious Queen's Award for Export Achievement. The award itself was presented to her by the Lord Lieutenant of London at a private party at Claridge's Hotel, which included a retrospective of her work. She is justly proud of this achievement and even today she maintains a high percentage of sales abroad. Following the presentation, Elizabeth attended a party at Buckingham Palace. After being presented to The Queen and The Duke of Edinburgh, she had the chance to meet other winners and to talk to the royal couple.

20 Albemarle Street remained Elizabeth Gage's only retail outlet for 20 years until 2004, when The Royal Institution of Great Britain, which owned the freehold, decided to activate a break clause in the lease in order to open a restaurant for their members and visitors. By way of recompense to an exemplary tenant, The Royal Institution offered (and Elizabeth accepted) a new lease on a shop unit two doors down at 18 Albemarle Street, which it also happened to own. Meanwhile, Palm Beach was added to New York, Chicago, San Francisco, Dallas and Houston as a regular location for her exhibitions. This enabled Elizabeth's American clientele to continue growing and, of course, they would show up at the shop whenever visiting London.

Business was further aided by a robust world economy and, in particular, strong economic growth in the United States, where GDP typically held above 4% with only one brief contraction in 1991. A scheme (sadly no longer in place at the time of writing) whereby overseas clients could export purchases made in the UK back to their home country thus avoiding the necessity to pay VAT was also hugely beneficial to retailers of luxury goods, especially in London.

18 Albemarle Street remained open until 2012, when Elizabeth decided to consolidate her operations at 5 West Halkin Street, Knightsbridge – a building close to her London home that had housed the administrative offices and workshops where her pieces had

The showroom at 5 West Halkin Street, London SW1. [© Elizabeth Gage Ltd]

been made since 1990. Here, a new showroom was opened on the ground floor where, today, clients can view the jewels or, if they prefer, collect pieces they have chosen online.

Shortly after the opening of the new showroom at West Halkin Street, Zoë Simpson announced her retirement as company secretary, triggering the search for a replacement. Serendipity once again intervened in the shape of Joanne Rees, introduced by a mutual friend, who joined the company. Joanne, an experienced sales and marketing executive, quickly recognised that the business processes in place had been designed for a different era and needed to adapt to the way clients now preferred to shop for jewellery. She undertook an immediate strategic review of the company and implemented a modernisation plan. Joanne Rees was appointed Managing Director in 2017 and remains Elizabeth Gage's closest and most valued business associate to this day.

Awards and Accolades

In her 60-year career as a jewellery designer, Elizabeth has achieved many special awards and public accolades. Her Cartier commission was a startling achievement for a young jeweller barely out of college in the late 1960s. Her De Beers Diamonds International Award in 1972 and Queen's Award for Export Achievement in 1989 acknowledged an exceptional level of accomplishment both as a creative force and as a businesswoman. More recently, since the turn of the millennium, three further landmark achievements have given Elizabeth immense pride and satisfaction.

In 2008, Elizabeth Gage was presented with the prestigious Lifetime Achievement Award by leading jewellery magazine *Retail Jeweller* at a gala ceremony at the Grosvenor House Hotel in London. The award is not an annual event and is only given when someone is recognised as having made a major contribution to the UK's jewellery industry. Sarah Carpin, then Editor of *Retail Jeweller*, presented the award and gave a speech in which she remarked that Elizabeth was one of the most respected and influential designers of her generation.

Then, in 2015, a retrospective of Elizabeth's work was shown at the New Britain Museum of American Art in Connecticut. 'The Enchanting Jewels of Elizabeth Gage', which ran from 26 April to 26 July, showcased approximately 250 pieces of fine jewellery, spanning the 50 years of her career. Each item in the exhibition had been hand-picked by Elizabeth Gage and included works from her own archive as well as from the private collections of clients from around the world. It seems remarkable that a museum dedicated strictly to American art chose to 'adopt' a British jewellery designer (albeit with an American mother). The fact that they did so bears testament to the high regard in which they viewed her artistry.

Two years later, in the summer of 2017, Elizabeth was named in The Queen's Birthday Honours List to receive an MBE, which was presented to her at the investiture ceremony at Buckingham Palace on Thursday 16 November. The award was given in recognition of her services to the British jewellery industry and in many ways represents her most treasured accomplishment in a career now spanning seven decades. On receiving the news, Elizabeth expressed her delight and gratitude, saying: 'I am honoured and extremely proud to receive such an award for my work. I feel so privileged to have been able to make my career doing what I love. This is a very special moment in my life and one which I will always cherish.'

Clientele

Thus far little mention has been made of clients. Over the years there have been many, including a fair number of household names, though modesty and discretion forbids their disclosure. There are, however, two notable friends and patrons (neither is still living) who may be divulged.

The first is Fleur Cowles, the American painter, writer and renowned society hostess who lived with her fourth (and last) husband Tom Montague Meyer in Albany, Piccadilly. It was Fleur Cowles 'the artist' who befriended Elizabeth Gage and recognised in her a fellow artist and kindred spirit. She was not, oddly enough, a prolific buyer of jewellery but did

Elizabeth Gage receiving her MBE from The King (then The Prince of Wales) in 2017. [Photo: British Ceremonial Arts]

Opposite: The 'Tom Pin' (2001), which was commissioned by Fleur Cowles. [@ Elizabeth Gage Ltd]

commission Elizabeth to design her Tom Pin – a lion's head carved from fossilised palm and framed in a halo of golden leaves. The pin is based on a picture Cowles painted for the cover of Robert Vavra's book *Tiger Flower*.

Fleur Cowles edited and penned the foreword to Elizabeth Gage's autobiography *The Unconventional Gage*, published in 2003. In it, Cowles writes: 'Since I came to London, I have never given up either an alert eye or inspiration for tomorrow's genius; I've kept looking for artistic talent. For this reason, I was immensely excited when I came across the unique work of Elizabeth Gage who brings colour and beauty into my world. I give this accolade to a dear and amazingly gifted friend.' The friendship lasted until Fleur Cowles's death, aged 101, in 2009.

The second notable friend and patron was another American, the actress Lauren Bacall, who wandered into the shop at 20 Albemarle Street in 1985. Bacall was in London playing the lead in the Pinter-directed Tennessee Williams play, *Sweet Bird of Youth*, at the nearby Haymarket Theatre.

Bacall adored jewellery and, unlike Fleur Cowles, she owned a lot of it. Over the next two decades, their relationship flourished, and Bacall purchased nearly two dozen jewels from Elizabeth Gage. Perhaps her most treasured piece was the Moghul-inspired Camel Pin, commissioned in 1990. The inception of the brooch was initiated by Bacall when she presented Elizabeth with an Indian bejewelled gold chess piece in the shape of a camel and asked her to convert it into a wearable piece of jewellery.

Elizabeth obliged by setting the camel on top of an elaborate gold and foliate enamelled Jaipur plaque enhanced with diamonds and a drop pearl. In 2015, the Camel Pin was auctioned by Bonhams, New York, in their Lauren Bacall Collection sale for over four times the pre-sale estimate.

Opposite: Lauren Bacall wears her 'Camel Pin' at the Waldorf Astoria Hotel, New York, in 1990 [© Ron Galella, Ltd / Ron Galella Collection via Getty Images]

CHAPTER 4
Collections

Previous page: Elizabeth Gage in 1985. [Courtesy of Elizabeth Gage]

Persian Carpet Agincourt Ring (2023). Rubellite cabochons, golden citrines, green tourmalines and sapphires set in yellow gold. The distinctive Agincourt design includes a foxtail chain running through loops along the ring's edge, offering a unique and flexible wearing experience. Elizabeth Gage collection. [© Elizabeth Gage Ltd]

This chapter gathers together a representative selection of Elizabeth Gage jewels organised into themes and spanning the length of her career as a designer. Much of the associated commentary has been set down in Elizabeth's own words. Such is her passion, eloquence and erudition when describing her designs and the stories behind them that it is unnecessary to elaborate on what she has already written...her words are clearly expressed and obviously derived from heartfelt personal experience.

The Classics

Many of Elizabeth Gage's most popular and enduring designs have been informed by medieval and renaissance history – subjects that have captured her imagination since she was a child. It is not just the style of jewellery people wore in ancient times but also the pageantry, heraldry, heroes and legends associated with those times that she so enjoys weaving into her art. On the following pages is an assortment of these classic pieces together with Elizabeth's explanation of the fascinating history and inspiration behind some of them.

Agincourt

'One of the earliest pieces I made at Sir John Cass College was a ring, set with amethysts and peridots. I wanted it to look like a modern drum, but when finished it resembled a Persian carpet. I called it my Agincourt ring.

'I won a De Beers Award five years later for another style of Agincourt ring. Each section had a half-carat diamond, set in deeply carved gold, divided by tiny pavé-set diamonds.

'The iconic Agincourt ring is made in articulated sections and finished with a foxtail chain, making it not only beautiful to look at but also flexible and comfortable to wear. It has therefore justifiably become one of our most popular and enduring designs.'

Above: Tapered Agincourt Ring with Tanzanite (2024). Yellow gold set with a faceted round tanzanite and featuring articulated sections decorated with carved gold triangles. Elizabeth Gage collection. [© Elizabeth Gage Ltd]

Right: Agincourt Friendship Ring (2022). Yellow gold featuring five white-gold oak leaf motifs pavé-set with 56 brilliant-cut diamonds. Elizabeth Gage collection. [© Elizabeth Gage Ltd]

Sagittarius and Diamond Zodiac Tapered Ring (2019). Yellow gold featuring the Sagittarius sign with sun, moon and planet motifs and decorated with eight brilliant-cut diamonds. Elizabeth Gage collection. [@ Elizabeth Gage Ltd]

Opposite, left: Aquamarine Tapered Templar Ring (2024). Yellow gold set with a round aquamarine cabochon and decorated with a chevron pattern in blue enamel. Elizabeth Gage collection. [@ Elizabeth Gage Ltd]

Opposite, right: Diamond and Enamel Templar Band Ring (1974). Yellow gold decorated with blue and red enamel and twisted gold wire and set with four round brilliant-cut diamonds. Elizabeth Gage collection. [@ Elizabeth Gage Ltd]

Zodiac

'My zodiac story started purely by chance. In 1964, whilst visiting the Benaki Museum in Athens, I came upon a long cylinder decorated by many lion heads. It so inspired me, that I made a ring with four lions' heads set around a band. A friend immediately asked if I would make one for her, with her star sign, so my lion became a Leo, and eleven other Signs of the Zodiac quickly followed.'

Templar

'Following the success of my Zodiac rings, I went on to create the Templar ring, naming it after the Knights Templar (the first Bankers in Europe). The ring has an architectural quality about it, similar to the banners and pageantry of the 14th century.

'The Knights Templar are believed to have guarded the way to the Holy Land through Europe. However, the Pope, Clement V, and the French King, Philippe le Bel, turned against them and accused them of heresy. They were jealous of the wealth of the Knights Templar and, therefore, their power.

'In 1307, on Friday 13 October, both the King and the Pope plotted to arrest every Templar in France. This is the little-known background to our superstitions about this date and why it is considered to be so unlucky. Many of the Knights Templar did escape arrest but the Order was decimated and their Grand Master, Jacques de Molay, was tragically burnt at the stake in 1314.

'In order to make a Templar ring, the stones are placed around in various shapes and sizes to create balance and harmony between the width of the ring, the size of the stones and the style of the settings. For my Templar rings, I use rub-over settings as opposed to claw settings. Firstly, because that gives the correct look to the ring and makes a statement with each stone and, secondly, I see these rings as jewellery women can wear every day, and these settings will not catch on clothing.

'I have designed this ring in so many different variations and even now, years later, I can create new motifs and symbols for them. The Templar ring can be worn first thing in the morning and hold its own at a very grand dinner – a versatile ring that can be either simple or detailed.'

Left: Mint Green Tourmaline Charlemagne Ring (2023). Large oval mint-green tourmaline set in a yellow-gold bombé shank; the gallery is adorned with six additional mint-green tourmalines and eight brilliant-cut diamonds. Elizabeth Gage collection. [© Elizabeth Gage Ltd]

Below: Sapphire and Red Spinel Charlemagne Ring (2024). Polished yellow gold, an oval faceted sapphire in a surround of 11 red spinel carved-leaf cameos; the gallery is decorated with groups of three round faceted sapphires alternating with carved gold plinths. Elizabeth Gage collection. [© Elizabeth Gage Ltd]

Charlemagne

'History has always influenced my work. The characters are always interesting – in particular, the Emperor Charlemagne. I had never seen such a beautiful jewel as the one called Charlemagne's Talisman, which can now be seen in the Palais du Tau in Reims. It has a very pale sapphire with a section of the True Cross placed behind it and is surrounded by beautiful stones. The jewel is opulent and magnificent, yet incredibly simple, which to me is how jewellery should be.

'My contemporary Charlemagne rings are meant to be a tribute to the rare beauty of the original jewel. There is really no end to the variation of design that I can create around the central stone, and it remains a simple concept with a splendour that never fails to draw a great deal of attention, whether it is pavéd with diamonds or enamelled in glorious colour.

'The Charlemagne ring is still one of the most important rings that I make and continues to be one of my favourites.'

Crown

'My fascination with France continued after the Charlemagne and Templar periods, and next came the Renaissance. I have great feeling and understanding for this period: the houses that people built, their clothes, their jewellery, the pictures they painted and the gardens they designed.

'I was inspired by the magnificent royal crowns, whose dazzling stones simply take your breath away. Any woman would love to receive a crown from the one she loves. My crown rings are pure romance.'

Diamond Crown Ring (2019). Yellow gold and diamonds. The central band is decorated with gold bead clusters and eight round diamonds set inside square plinths; the outer bands are each adorned with gold beads and four brilliant-cut diamonds. Elizabeth Gage collection. [© Elizabeth Gage Ltd]

Left: Mandarin Garnet Heliotrope Ring (2023). Large, intensely coloured mandarin garnet and 16 brilliant-cut diamonds set in yellow gold. Elizabeth Gage collection. [© Elizabeth Gage Ltd]

Below: Blue Cat's-Eye Tourmaline Heliotrope Ring (2023). Yellow gold decorated with teal-coloured enamel and gold crescent moon and ankh motifs and set with a large and rare blue cat's eye tourmaline cabochon and two brilliant-cut diamonds. Elizabeth Gage collection. [© Elizabeth Gage Ltd]

Heliotrope

'I adore these bright purple flowers and also the name, which translated from ancient Greek means "turns toward the sun". In classical mythology, recounted by Ovid in his narrative poem *Metamorphoses*, the water nymph Clytie falls in love with the sun-god Helios and is betrayed by him. Wasting away, she transforms into the heliotrope, whose flowers always face the sun.'

Kiss

'Earrings add the finishing touch to a face. Different shapes suit different individuals, so to me the shape of the face always dictates the style of the earring. At first, I thought that making earrings would be an easy step after rings, but I quickly realised the enormity of the task because every woman has unique ears. As a designer, I had to allow for pierced ears, large or dainty lobes and the angle from which the earrings are seen. An exciting challenge.

'In the 18th century, for evening wear, ladies favoured diamond and pearl earrings, as this stylish combination instantly lit up their faces in candlelight. Blue sapphires tended to be too dark and therefore yellow sapphires and pink spinels were the gemstones of choice because they held their colour at night.

'I began with a simple pearl and diamond earring – the Kiss – and in the following pages I will take you through my journey from this very first pair.'

Clockwise from top left:
Amethyst and Grey Pearl Kiss Pin (2005). Yellow gold set with a large cushion-shaped amethyst and four oval chequerboard-cut amethysts topped with gold beads; four natural-grey Akoya pearls are held in fluted gold caps decorated with green enamel. Elizabeth Gage collection. [© Elizabeth Gage Ltd]

Pearl and Diamond Kiss Earrings (2001). Yellow gold with a central white Mabé pearl and four smaller pearls interspersed with diamond crescents pavé-set in white gold with four old-cut diamonds nestled within the crescent. Elizabeth Gage collection. [© Elizabeth Gage Ltd]

Kiss Earrings with Rubellites, Pearls and Amethysts (2024). Yellow gold, vibrant oval, faceted rubellites encircled by amethyst beads set in beaded gold caps interspersed with cultured plume pearls. Elizabeth Gage collection. [© Elizabeth Gage Ltd]

Left: Leopard Jasper African Queen Earrings (2018). Yellow gold, leopard jasper cabochons surrounded by twisted gold wire, topped with a brilliant-cut diamond set in a square gold plinth, and three carnelian beads at the base. Elizabeth Gage collection. [© Elizabeth Gage Ltd]

Below: Kunzite African Queen Earrings (2018). Oval kunzites framed in a polished yellow-gold surround with three round kunzites at the base. Elizabeth Gage collection. [© Elizabeth Gage Ltd]

African Queen

'After I had created the Kiss earring it became clear that it was indeed African in origin – I had been subconsciously influenced by African neck rings, the spirals of gold. The incredible beauty of the beaten gold has a life of its own and is made with a great deal of love and tradition.

'I married this first earring with my Templar style and created the African Queen earring which has been a constant success.'

Hematite African Queen Earrings (2021). Oval cabochon hematite set in a twisted gold wire surround, topped with a diamond set in a square gold plnth. Three grey baroque cultured pearls held in wire caps form the base. Elizabeth Gage collection. [© Elizabeth Gage Ltd]

Valois

'The House of Valois ruled the Kingdom of France during the late medieval period from 1328 to 1589. After holding the throne for over 200 years, the Valois male line died out and the House of Bourbon succeeded to the French throne.

'The Valois dynasty owned huge collections of decorative metalwork as well as jewels ("joyaux") for personal adornment. These pieces were made largely from gold in the gothic style. Jewellery at this time was restricted to those from aristocratic and noble houses, with laws prohibiting commoners from wearing "joaillerie" with precious stones and pearls – hence the distinction between "joaillerie" and "bijouterie", which still exists in France today. I love the style of this period and am in awe of the craftsmanship deployed in its making.'

Clockwise from top left:

Bronze Coin Molten Gold Ring (2022). A bronze coin depicting Flavius Julius Constans (Roman Emperor, 337–350 CE) set in molten yellow gold. Elizabeth Gage collection. [© Elizabeth Gage Ltd]

Hugs & Kisses Ring (2014). Yellow gold, 36 round brilliant-cut diamonds set in alternating hugs and kisses motifs. Elizabeth Gage collection. [© Elizabeth Gage Ltd]

Dolphin Ring (2020). Two yellow-gold dolphin heads with cabochon sapphire eyes and rose-cut diamonds along their necks. Elizabeth Gage collection. [© Elizabeth Gage Ltd]

Gold Jewellery

More simple styles of jewellery for everyday use have been perennial favourites with Elizabeth Gage's clients. Typically made in yellow gold and sometimes embellished with the odd pearl or diamond, these are jewels to throw on in the morning, which can be worn with almost anything. They become a part of the wearer's personal identity, and, in many instances, she doesn't feel 'properly dressed' without them.

Left: Shiraz Earrings (2020). Yellow gold with granulated and gold wire detailing, brilliant-cut diamonds and white Akoya drop pearls. Elizabeth Gage collection. [© Elizabeth Gage Ltd]

Below: Gold Bark Bracelet (2024). An articulated yellow gold bracelet featuring 24 individual sections with a textured bark finish. Elizabeth Gage collection. [© Elizabeth Gage Ltd]

Chalcedony Cufflinks (2018). Chalcedony cabochons in a molten yellow-gold surround, molten gold swivel-bar backs. Elizabeth Gage Collection. [© Elizabeth Gage Ltd]

Men's Jewellery

An important part of Elizabeth Gage's work is jewellery created for men. Gone are the days when fashionable dandies in the 18th century would adorn themselves with ornate buttons, fanciful shoe buckles and elaborate cane-heads. Neither are jewel-encrusted gold cases containing bespoke Turkish cigarettes much in demand today.

Fortunately, cufflinks and signet rings and the like are still worn by men who appreciate discreet personal adornment. Elizabeth Gage's first pair of Ram's Head cufflinks were made for Cartier in New York, and they have been a favourite ever since. She enjoys using enamel and molten gold and often incorporates coins or stones into her designs. Her Zodiac and Templar styles also translate well into cufflinks. Additionally, Elizabeth has undertaken special commissions from discerning contemporary 'dandies' with an appetite for statement style, resulting in the creation of many unique pieces of bespoke men's jewellery.

Coins and Artefacts

'Coins have always held a fascination for me because of their historical association. I find it interesting to learn about the lives of the people whose heads feature on the coins. I became fascinated by Alexander the Great after using coins bearing his head many times in my jewellery – he was so young to have captured the dedication and loyalty of his troops. When I pick up an ancient coin, I am aware that I am touching a piece that has been handled by people many hundreds of years ago. Once I made a bracelet with coins that had been in use at the time of Jesus. Historically they are of great importance.

'Coins have much information to give and were a very early form of advertising. For example, Thessaly – a region of Greece that was home to Achilles and Jason – would stamp the reverse of their coins with the image of beautiful horses. Athens would have an owl representing the Goddess Athena. Pegasus was identified with Corinth and the coastal town of Tarentum – a Roman city on the "heel" of Italy – chose a boy on a dolphin. The image of a gate for any city would commemorate a famous victory. Coins were, therefore, an early form of propaganda created for the victors.

'To me, money is an energy to be used for good as well as bad. Coins are a connection with the past: perhaps some have been used to buy groceries or to pay a king's ransom. And why were they left buried in huge hoards? Were the owners fleeing? Did they think they would collect them later?

'The first time I used a coin, the goldsmith showed me the finished gleaming coin, which he had polished until it shone – thereby removing two thousand years of patina! I was devastated.

'Artefacts have a similar appeal to coins because of their historical importance. Certain periods interest me, particularly the early Celtic, Viking and medieval periods, probably because they were associated with Britain as well as Europe.

'I take great care in sourcing my artefacts, as I prefer to know as much as possible about the provenance of each piece. Each artefact that I buy has its own special story and this often influences my design. A charming example is a Roman lady who held her cloak in place with a bronze rabbit brooch. Eighteen hundred years later I designed a set of rabbit pins to be worn by the modern woman.

'Amongst the artefacts I have used are fragments of shields, decorations from horse bridles and amulets from the 3rd and 4th centuries BCE. Each acts as a talisman, bringing the wearer good luck. They are all intriguing as they have come from an earlier original piece.

'Although not strictly an artefact, I like to tell a story about the most incredible piece of turquoise I have ever seen – a long rectangular stone whose beauty took my breath away. It belonged to a friend. She requested that I hold the stone and describe what I felt. An unusual request as I do not usually interpret stones in this way.

'I told her I felt a beat pulsing through the stone, and she explained that it had once belonged to a great Sioux Chief who wore it round his neck, resting against his beating heart.'

This page, clockwise from top left:

Cuff bracelet (2000). The central ancient coin, which features the personification of Constantinopolis (Constantinople; now Istanbul in Turkey) is encircled by a wide carnelian frame, set in textured yellow gold with a surface impression taken from a coin. Private collection, California, USA. [© Elizabeth Gage Ltd]

The Antoninus Pin (1995). A Roman coin with a yellow-gold surround decorated with eau-de-nil enamel, surmounted with a carved chalcedony head. The central coin was found in the old Roman town of Cirencester, England in the 1980s, and bears the image of Antoninus Pius, Roman Emperor from 138 to 161 CE. Private collection, New York, USA. [© Elizabeth Gage Ltd]

The Icarus Pin (1989). A Roman bronze head (2nd to 3rd century CE) found in Tunisia mounted on a textured yellow gold body with a cabochon ruby heart; a coin of Carausius, a 3rd century military commander of the Roman Empire, is set below. The jewel, so golden and molten in appearance, suggested the name: Icarus. Private collection, New Jersey, USA. [© Elizabeth Gage Ltd]

Opposite: The Dalmatian Necklace (2000). Dalmatian jasper beads and yellow gold. At the centre of the pendant is a Roman bronze follis – a type of coin in the Roman and Byzantine tradition – (circa 30 CE) with the profile of Emperor Constantine the Great set in a circle of molten yellow gold. Private collection, California, USA. [© Elizabeth Gage Ltd]

The Noble Mariner (1988). A large and very rare gold ryal coin of Edward IV (reigned 1461–83), surrounded by gold-set diamonds and mabé pearls with a large, irregular cabochon fluorite drop. The coin, also known as a rose noble, features the King in armour, standing in a ship facing forwards, hence: 'The Noble Mariner'. Elizabeth Gage Archive. [© Elizabeth Gage Ltd]

Opposite: The Hollandia Necklace (1999). A Silver Ducat in a yellow-gold frame suspended from twisted rows of strung pale aquamarine beads with yellow gold funnels. The centrepiece of the pendant is a Dutch silver ducat, minted in 1576, which was travelling on *The Hollandia* when the vessel sank in a storm in 1743. The necklace was aptly purchased by a lady named Narissa, which means 'sea nymph' and stems from the Nereides, who in Greek mythology were goddesses of the sea and protectors of sailors and fishermen. Private collection, California, USA. [© Elizabeth Gage Ltd]

Mary Tudor Pin (1989). Mary I silver coin (minted in 1554) set in a yellow-gold surround decorated with rubies and diamonds, surmounted by a brilliant-cut brown tourmaline; at the base, separated by a gold and diamond-set hinge capped with pearls, is a larger chequerboard-cut brown tourmaline. Private collection, New York, USA. [© Elizabeth Gage Ltd]

Opposite: The Armenian Pin (1990). An Armenian silver coin (12th–13th century CE) framed in yellow gold and topped with a diamond-set square plinth; below the coin are two bi-colour tourmaline slices connected by an onyx triangle; the pin is finished with a baroque pearl drop. Photographed with a matching pair of earrings. Private collection. [© Elizabeth Gage Ltd]

Cycladic Head Pin (1988). A white marble Cycladic head (circa 4,000–4,500 BCE) with carved yellow-gold collar and chest set with a small cabochon ruby; the head is topped with three gold beads. Elizabeth Gage Archive. [© Elizabeth Gage Ltd]

Opposite: The Alexander Necklace (1989). A silver Alexander I coin in a gold surround suspended from a necklace of twisted hematite beads with molten gold funnels. Photographed with complementary ring and earrings. Private collection. [© Elizabeth Gage Ltd]

The Running Lion Pin (1992). An Eastern Mediterranean bronze lion (1st–2nd century CE, probably originally used on a shield) embellished with a yellow-gold saddle and harness studded with diamonds and rubies; the saddle is fringed with pearls. His golden boots are to prevent him from scratching the wearer! Private collection, London, UK. [© Elizabeth Gage Ltd]

Opposite: Minoan Seal Pin (1967). Ancient steatite (soapstone) intaglio seals from Crete framed in twisted yellow-gold wire; Baroque pearls provide lustre and contrast. Photographed with matching earrings made in 1970. These early designs would later evolve into the iconic Kiss Pin and African Queen Earrings. V&A, London. [© Elizabeth Gage Ltd]

The Bucephalus Pin (1997). A 19th-century russet glass intaglio of Alexander the Great portrayed as Hercules set in a gold surround decorated with red and black enamel; a Romano-British bronze horse (2nd century CE) sits at the top, decorated with its original enamelling. Elizabeth Gage named the pin after Alexander's horse, Bucephalus. Private collection, Illinois, USA. [© Elizabeth Gage Ltd]

Opposite: The Snowflake Necklace (2000). A yellow-gold pendant, with a silver coin of Demeter (circa 350 BCE), suspended from a necklace of rock crystal beads with 'snowflake' inclusions. Demeter was the Greek goddess who symbolised Mother Earth. She was also the mother of Persephone, the goddess of spring, who was abducted by Hades and became queen of the underworld. Photographed with complementary ring and earrings. Private collection, California, USA. [© Elizabeth Gage Ltd]

The Ampulla Pin (1992). Early Christian ampoule for Holy Water (8th–9th century CE) framed in molten yellow-gold wire, with a cabachon turquoise on the collar and crowned with a brilliant-cut diamond. The piece is completed with a Mexican fire opal drop. Photographed with complementary ring and earrings. Private collection, Texas, USA. [© Elizabeth Gage Ltd]

Opposite: Flight of the Dragon Pin (1997). A Celtic dragon figure (circa 50 BCE) flies above a yellow-gold sun disc set with a Roman bronze amulet (2nd–3rd century CE). Photographed with a selection of Royal Crown rings. Private collection, France. [© Elizabeth Gage Ltd]

Rufus Pin (2000). A Viking bronze figure resembling a small dog (circa 800 CE) surrounded by diamonds set in granulated yellow gold, topped with a mandarin garnet. Private collection, Georgia, USA.
[© Elizabeth Gage Ltd]

Opposite: Celtic Horse Pendant (1997). A bronze horse head, possibly a fragment of an ancient Celtic knife handle, decorated with yellow gold, resting on a large, beaten-gold bead; the pendant hangs from a matching gold tube necklace. Private collection France. [© Elizabeth Gage Ltd]

Three Rabbit Pins (1994). A Romano-bronze rabbit (3rd or 4th century CE) sits atop each of these enamelled gold pins. Such animal brooches were popular with the Romans and have been found at sites all over England. The centrepiece of the top pin is a 16th-century farm token made of lead; these were given to farm workers instead of money to be exchanged for food or goods. The bottom two pins feature snail shells carved from green tourmaline and fire opal. Various private collections. [© Elizabeth Gage Ltd]

Opposite: The Karnak Necklace (1988). A large Egyptian faience (tin-glazed) scarab framed in yellow gold and decorated with blue enamel 'rays' hangs from a necklace of granulated gold links interspersed with blue coral beads and two faience ankhs. The scarab and the ankh are symbols of rebirth and eternal life. Elizabeth Gage Archive. [© Elizabeth Gage Ltd]

Left: Janus Heads Ring (1988). A yellow-gold Charlemagne ring set with an 18th-century blue glass intaglio by master engraver James Tassie. The gallery has round diamonds set into square gold plinths alternating with white enamel trellis patterns. Elizabeth Gage Archive. [© Elizabeth Gage Ltd]

Opposite: Tassie Kiss Pin (1988). Yellow gold set with clear glass intaglios by James Tassie; the central oval intaglio features a red enamel surround. The diagonals are set with carved onyx 'fruits' in gold wire funnels decorated with diamonds in carved gold plinths. Photographed with matching earrings. Private collection, Washington, D.C., USA. [© Elizabeth Gage Ltd]

Intaglios and Cameos

'In the mid-1980s I began to incorporate intaglios and cameos into my jewellery because I loved their colour and definition. There is a simple difference between an intaglio and a cameo. An intaglio is cut so that the engraving goes into the stone, whilst a cameo is carved in relief.

'When the Grand Tour was fashionable (during the 18th and 19th centuries), intaglio stones in carnelian, agate, sapphire and emerald, to name but a few, would be brought home and incorporated into a collection, rather like stamp collectors do today. Some great collectors in the 19th century kept their original stone intaglios carefully hidden away, showing glass replicas to protect against loss or theft of the original. The process used by James Tassie (the 18th-century Scottish engraver) to make his vitreous paste for imitation gemstones has now been lost. An Italian firm today makes glass intaglios, but the colours are very different from the originals.

'I found some 19th-century clear glass intaglios that were engraved with cupids, love letters and roses, which allowed me to create some lovely pins around them. A favourite was a cherub playing a flute to a butterfly with the words "La musique enchante l'âme" ("music enchants the soul"). Roses were often accompanied by the words "Thy sweetness is my life" or "Tho' lost to sight, to memory clear". These intaglios were normally given to friends and loved ones, as a gesture of affection.

'It has always interested me how popular intaglios and cameos have been in the past, especially in 19th-century France. During the Napoleonic era, almost every lady of fashion wore an arm band, necklace, pair of earrings or some item of jewellery with a cameo in it. Using a cameo, old or new, has always been a delight for me as they provide a central theme for a piece of jewellery.'

Left: The Noble Youth Pin (1996). An 18th-century Intaglio in black glass by James Tassie and (below) a modern intaglio of a phoenix carved in fossilised wood, both framed in yellow gold and connected via gold bead cups topped with carnelians. Private collection, Massachusetts, USA. [© Elizabeth Gage Ltd]

Below: The Head in the Clouds Pin (1999). An intaglio carved from sunstone and set in layers of yellow gold and enamel. The piece is further decorated with diamonds pavé set in white gold. Photographed with matching enamel earrings with diamonds pavé set in white and yellow gold. Private collection, Massachusetts, USA. [© Elizabeth Gage Ltd]

Opposite: The Muse Pin (1996). Yellow gold, central cushion-shaped aquamarine intaglio of a lady playing a lyre, surrounded by alternating triangular cabochon aquamarines and cultured plume-shaped pearls. Photographed with a complementary Templar ring and shell cluster earrings. Private collection, Michigan, USA. [© Elizabeth Gage Ltd]

Top left: Arcadia Pin (2000). Rock crystal intaglios depicting a Roman emperor and a bee, each set within a beaten yellow-gold surround topped with a diamond plinth; the intaglios are separated by cultured South Sea silver baroque pearls in beaded funnels. Private collection, Missouri, USA.

Bottom left: Cameo Pin (1999). Agate cameo of a classical lady, surrounded by repoussé yellow gold, with diamond-set flower motifs to each quarter. Private collection, Florida, USA. [© Elizabeth Gage Ltd]

Opposite: Phoenix Pendant Necklace (1987). An oval emerald cameo of a phoenix framed in granulated yellow gold with an oval cabochon aquamarine at its base. The pendant is suspended from a necklace of twisted emerald and aquamarine beads terminating in granulated yellow-gold funnels. Photographed with a complementary blue topaz ring and yellow gold 'Wing' earrings. Private collection, California, USA. [© Elizabeth Gage Ltd]

This page, clockwise from top left:

Rubellite Cameo Ring (1999). A carved rubellite cameo set in yellow gold, with a white enamel trellis gallery and four oval pink sapphires. Private collection, Massachusetts, USA. [© Elizabeth Gage Ltd]

The January Pin (1998). A cameo carved in jasper depicting the two-faced Roman god Janus, ruler of the month of January. The head looking backwards is that of an old man and the one looking forwards, a youth. The surround is decorated with four citrines set in square gold plinths on a mango-coloured enamel background; oak leaves, with brown enamel detail are scattered in between. Private collection, New South Wales, Australia. [© Elizabeth Gage Ltd]

The Tudor Lion Pin (1995). The head of a lion carved in yellow beryl and framed inside a fluid line of yellow gold; the finishing touch is a diamond star in the centre of his forehead. Below, separated by pearl-capped beaded gold cones, is a badge-shaped cameo of an English Tudor rose carved in deep red tourmaline. Private collection, Arizona, USA. [© Elizabeth Gage Ltd]

Opposite: Olympic Pin and Earrings (2000). Three antique cameos carved in agate of men wearing laurel and vine wreaths, in frames of eau-de-nil enamel decorated with yellow gold myrtle leaves and diamonds. The pin has a South Sea cultured baroque pearl at the base. Wreaths were awarded to the victors of athletic competitions in Ancient Greece; the laurel wreath is particularly associated with the god Apollo, who is commonly depicted wearing one. Elizabeth Gage Archive. [© Elizabeth Gage Ltd]

Left: Cameo Charlemagne Ring (2000). Yellow gold set with a grey and white agate cameo of a cherub, surrounded by four red spinels, gold beads and diamonds. Private collection, New York, USA. [© Elizabeth Gage Ltd]

Below: The Constanzia Necklace (1990). A contemporary cameo of a girl's head carved in emerald, framed in carved yellow gold and suspended from a necklace of red fossil beads. Emerald is associated with the goddess Venus and also the birthstone for May. Private collection, Houston, USA. [© Elizabeth Gage Ltd]

Opposite: Templar Knight Pendant (1991). A carnelian cameo of a Templar knight on horseback is suspended from a necklace of onyx beads linked by granulated-gold end caps. Photographed with a complementary scarab ring. Private collection, Switzerland. [© Elizabeth Gage Ltd]

Nature's Invasion

Left: The Birdsong Pin (2000). A carved bi-coloured tourmaline, depicting a blackbird with a jasper beak, sits within a yellow-gold and passion-fruit-coloured enamel frame topped with a diamond. Private collection, Connecticut, USA. [© Elizabeth Gage Ltd]

Right: The Cockerel Pin (1997). A cockerel carved from various jaspers and hand-painted in black enamel, framed within a hand-engraved yellow-gold feather. Private collection, Virginia, USA. [© Elizabeth Gage Ltd]

Opposite: The Talk of the Town Pin (1988). Two carved pink tourmaline cockatoos with yellow tourmaline crests kiss above a striking yellow citrine framed in diamonds; below is a detachable baroque South Sea pearl drop. The pendant is suspended from a single row of pink cultured pearls. Private collection, New York, USA. [© Elizabeth Gage Ltd]

'My love of nature stems from my early childhood and is now expressed in my garden and my protection of the animals that inhabit it. My wonderful gardener has taught me much about birds and their habits and I have a bird tray just outside the kitchen window where I can watch woodpeckers, great tits and thrushes as they come to feed.

'Living things have been portrayed in art since the beginning of time. The cave paintings in Southern France, depicting herds of deer and other creatures, show how closely man lived with nature and how important it was to him. Egyptian friezes show hunting and fishing, while images of birds, fish and fanciful dolphins grace the walls of the Cretan Palace of Knossos.

'My study of wildlife links directly to symbolism: the sly fox, the wise owl, the slow tortoise and the clever monkey all have particular attributes. Gods and goddesses of ancient Greece used creatures as symbols: Athena had the owl; Hercules, the lion; Venus, the swan; and Neptune, the seahorse. In Egypt, the gods (only half-human) were depicted with the heads of the various birds and animals that the Egyptians observed living on the banks of the Nile. The Chinese use animal symbols for their Zodiac, a cycle lasting twelve years instead of the Western world's twelve months.

'I have a great passion for my animal carvings, and I hope you will sense it in the pieces I have chosen on the following pages.'

Caesar Pin (2003). A carved tsavorite parrot's head, with Tahitian pearl beak and painted rock crystal eye, set inside two engraved yellow-gold feathers separated by an oval green beryl. Private collection, Massachusetts, USA. [© Elizabeth Gage Ltd]

Opposite: The Jewelled Nest Pin (2001). A hawk's head carved from petrified palm with a yellow agate and indicolite beak sits atop a blue tourmaline cameo of a bird landing in its nest; the cameo is framed in yellow gold with a brown enamel seaweed pattern. Private collection, Idaho, USA. [© Elizabeth Gage Ltd]

The Aquila Pin (1988). A partly carved tourmaline eagle's head with the original crystals left to form his neck feathers; the head is crowned with a gold-mounted baroque pearl. A Roman Constantine bronze coin forms the centrepiece of the carved, yellow-gold body and tail. The stylised upper feathers are in linen-texture white gold, set with pink tourmalines. Private collection, California, USA. [© Elizabeth Gage Ltd]

Opposite: The Scarab Templar Ring (1972). A large lapis lazuli scarab set in a wide, tapered, yellow-gold band with red enamel detailing, gold beads and square motifs. Photographed with complementary Agincourt earrings. Elizabeth Gage Archive. [© Elizabeth Gage Ltd]

The Pink Butterfly Necklace (1987). A carved bi-colour tourmaline slice in a light gold frame pavé-set with diamonds. The detachable pendant is suspended from a necklace of strung hematite beads with a yellow-gold clasp. Private collection, New York, USA. [@ Elizabeth Gage Ltd]

Opposite: The Scarab Necklace (1992). Seventeen carved carnelian scarabs, each framed in gold and capped by three gold beads, suspended from an articulated necklace of polished and granulated yellow gold ovals. (200 scarabs were carved in order to find 17 perfectly matched specimens.) Elizabeth Gage Archive. [@ Elizabeth Gage Ltd]

The Rams Bracelet (1968). Black horn embellished with twisted gold wire holding two yellow-gold rams' heads carved in Crete. Elizabeth Gage Archive. [© Elizabeth Gage Ltd]

Opposite: The Butterfly Pin (1984). Yellow gold wire, faceted round-cut rubies, marquise diamonds set in white gold, pavé-set diamonds and black enamel. Photographed with complementary ring and earrings. Private collection, Vermont, USA. [© Elizabeth Gage Ltd]

The Aslan Pin (1994). A bi-colour tourmaline carved into a lion's head with a yellow-gold collar studded with diamonds and rubies; hand-shaped yellow gold forms the body and tail, decorated with black enamel patterns; a South Sea pearl hangs from his body. Private collection, Florida, USA. [© Elizabeth Gage Ltd]

Opposite: Aesop's Fables Necklace (1995). A central circular chalcedony carving depicting the tale of the frogs who wanted a king; five carved chalcedony roller seals depict scenes from other Aesop fables, with setting and links in carved, granulated yellow gold. Elizabeth Gage Archive. [© Elizabeth Gage Ltd]

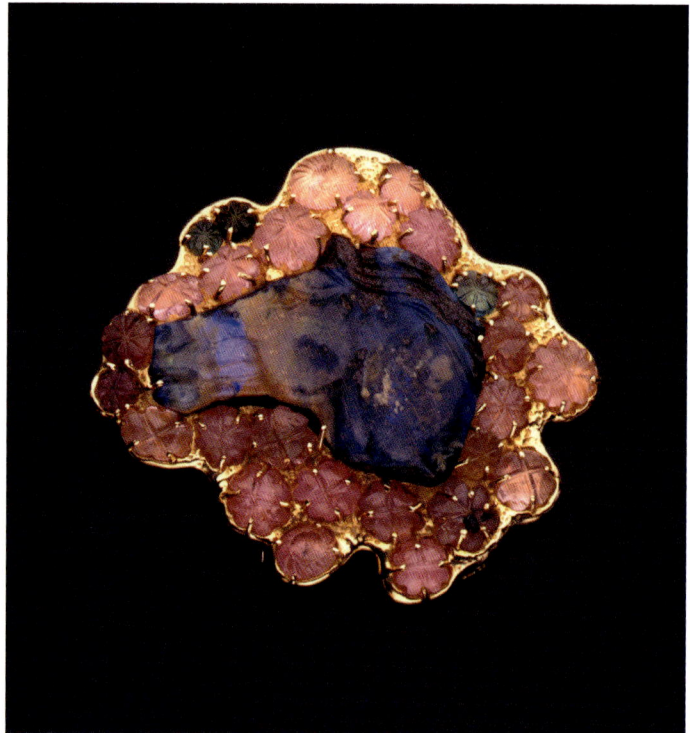

This page, clockwise from top left:

The Snow Leopard Pin (1998). A snow leopard's head, carved from petrified palm with a jasper nose and painted quartz eyes, rests inside a polished yellow-gold halo decorated with a brown enamel seaweed pattern and finished with a South Sea pearl. Private collection, Florida, USA. [@ Elizabeth Gage Ltd]

Snuffles (1990). A carved opal horse nuzzles pink and green tourmaline flowers, set in yellow gold. Elizabeth Gage Archive. [@ Elizabeth Gage Ltd]

The Safari Pin (2005). A leopard, carved from petrified palm, is draped over a carved jasper tree while it languishes in the dying African sun. It sits above a carved yellow tourmaline lion's head framed in beaten yellow gold and positioned between two carved jasper fruits. Private collection, Canada. [@ Elizabeth Gage Ltd]

Opposite: The Cheetah Pin (1988). A cheetah's head, carved from petrified palm, sits atop the yellow-gold base decorated with myrtle leaves and orange enamel. Set within the base is a brown glass intaglio by James Tassie depicting a classical man standing. Photographed with a matching pair of earring clips. Private collection, California, USA. [@ Elizabeth Gage Ltd]

Lion Earrings. Three sets of earrings featuring carved lion heads framed in yellow gold decorated with enamel. Top: Yellow tourmalines with black enamel seaweed (1998). Private collection, London, UK. Middle: Citrines with passion-fruit enamel and polished gold leaves (1998). Private collection, Georgia, USA. Bottom: Yellow tourmalines with red enamel seaweed (1997). Private collection, Connecticut, USA. [© Elizabeth Gage Ltd]

Opposite: The Kri-Kri Necklace (1981). The Kri-Kri (an ancient Cretan animal) depicted on this 22-carat yellow gold pendant was made using the impression of an ancient roller seal. It hangs from a large emerald bead attached to a necklace of twisted red jasper beads. Private collection, New York, USA. [© Elizabeth Gage Ltd]

Bear Cub Earrings (1995). Carved garnet bear cub heads set inside coiled, domed yellow gold frames decorated with black enamel triangles. Private collection, New York, USA. [@ Elizabeth Gage Ltd]

Opposite: The Carousel Horse Pin (1991). Carved in tourmaline and decorated with yellow gold, diamonds, rubies and pearl trappings. Private collection, North Carolina, USA. [@ Elizabeth Gage Ltd]

Jewels of the Sea

Above: Viking Ship Pin (1994). The yellow-gold boat, with a horse's head bow and a mermaid's tail stern, features a sail made from boulder opal, carved into a cameo of a salamander; plume-shaped cultured pearls adorn the pin, together a with a golden chain and diamonds. Private collection. [@ Elizabeth Gage Ltd]

Opposite: The Dolphin Pin (1975). A pair of golden dolphins adorned with diamonds and rubies touch noses in a swathe of tangled seaweed. Elizabeth Gage Archive. [@ Elizabeth Gage Ltd]

'The sea is a source of inspiration for all jewellers, especially to me. My very first major pin was the Dolphin. I went on to make a pair of shell cluster earrings that continue to sell today. Each pair is created by hand with unique variations – extra shells here, different ones there and diamonds scattered in diverse ways.

'My next plunge was into starfish pins. These most beautiful shapes are carved in aquamarine, coral, tourmaline and agate to name but a few. No two are ever the same, which gives me great personal excitement and is shared by my clients when they realise that they have something unique.

'Bracelets and rings followed in endless combinations. One of the earliest forms of sea-life was the ammonite, which lived in our oceans millions of years ago. It is now only found in fossilised form, but its shape has for centuries denoted the spiral of life and evolution. Fossils can be very difficult to work with as they can crumble easily, especially when being set. Smooth to the touch with extraordinary sandy, golden colours, ammonites have two sides that can be used: either its outside ridged surface or, when split in two, its inner surface. Ammonites appeal to me so much that I often have stones carved in the shape of them.'

The Spirit of the Sea Pin (2001). A sparkling dendrite agate starfish clings to a golden shell-encrusted rock, scattered with pavé-set diamonds. Private collection, Florida, USA. [@ Elizabeth Gage Ltd]

Opposite: The Spirit of Being Pin (2000). An exquisite black opal sits in a frame of polished and granulated yellow gold decorated with moons, stars and set with diamonds. Private collection, California, USA. [@ Elizabeth Gage Ltd]

The Delphini Pin (1991). A pair of exquisitely carved golden fish entwine their diamond-encrusted bodies around a pear-shaped pink tourmaline. Between their tails sits a baroque South Sea pearl, while a second pink tourmaline forms the drop. Private collection, New Jersey USA.
[© Elizabeth Gage Ltd]

Opposite: Ammonite Necklace (1987). An ammonite fossil, claw-set in a carved molten yellow-gold pendant, is suspended from a necklace of emerald beads with a wire and granulated gold clasp. Photographed with complementary pin and earrings. Private collection, New York, USA.
[© Elizabeth Gage Ltd]

The Mirror of Aphrodite Necklace (1989). A Roman bronze shell with grey pearl drop is suspended by a yellow gold chain from two carved pink tourmaline fish. Interspersed between the chain links sit six tiny, carved sapphire fish, each set in molten yellow gold. Photographed with matching earrings. Private collection, California, USA. [@ Elizabeth Gage Ltd]

Opposite: The Seahorse Pin (1992). A stylised seahorse dangles from a golden shell. His body, sculpted in yellow gold, is decorated with an array of different shaped blue and green tourmalines and finished with a baroque pearl and diamonds. Photographed with complementary ring and earrings. Private collection, Texas, USA. [@ Elizabeth Gage Ltd]

Sea Otter Pin (1998). Carved in green tourmaline, a sea otter emerges from a bed of seaweed floating on a shimmering gold surface. A baroque South Sea pearl provides the finishing touch. Photographed with complementary earrings. Private Collection, Massachusetts, USA. [© Elizabeth Gage Ltd]

Opposite: The Neptune Necklace (1988). A magnificent carved Australian boulder opal, depicting Neptune and his queen riding the waves on a shell pulled by seahorses, set in a yellow-gold frame decorated with diamonds and rubies with a baroque pearl drop. The necklace of black Tahitian pearls is linked together by gold caps set with rubies. Private collection, New York, USA. [© Elizabeth Gage Ltd]

Left: The Poseidon Pin (1996). Soft pink coral, engraved with the image of a young Poseidon, framed in beaten yellow gold atop a white shell and two pearls. Private collection, London, UK. [© Elizabeth Gage Ltd]

Below: The Rock Pool Pin (1988). A carved aquamarine pebble, held in place by fronds of gold seaweed, is set amongst a cluster of golden shells studded with diamonds, amethysts and a peridot. The plumes are carved from amethyst, green tourmaline and aquamarine. Photographed with complementary ring and earrings. Private collection, UK. [© Elizabeth Gage Ltd]

Opposite: The Aguilla Pin (1996). Carved aquamarine shells, one polished, the other unpolished, are set amongst golden shells entwined with seaweed and scattered with diamonds. Photographed with matching earrings. Private collection, New York, USA. [© Elizabeth Gage Ltd]

A Jewelled Garden

Above: The Old School House and garden. Elizabeth Gage's country home in Wiltshire and the inspiration for many of her nature themed designs.
[© Tom Greenly @ Greenly Photography]

Opposite: The Acanthus Leaf Pin (1992). A copper Charles I farthing (known as a 'Rose Farthing') is centred in a granulated yellow-gold acanthus leaf with a baroque South Sea pearl drop. Elizabeth Gage Archive. [© Elizabeth Gage Ltd]

'Although I live in London during the week, my great joy is my country home. Built in 1820, it is styled after a Greek basilica and was originally a Church school.

'The rose is one of my passions and I have different gardens surrounding the house filled with as many varieties as possible. There is a "potager" where I grow vegetables and fruit trees and I also have a "wild" garden designed around an old apple tree that has fallen over but, happily, is still alive.

'I have always been fascinated by leaf shapes. A favourite is myrtle for its simplicity as well as for its symbolism. It was sacred to the Goddess Aphrodite and was believed to bring good luck in marriage. Both the oak and vine leaf have been used symbolically for centuries. The oak, for example, is associated with kings and kingship, faith and courage. The oak garland was originally given to soldiers who had rescued a prisoner, but later, was used for any act of courage on the battlefield.

'The vine, obviously associated with Bacchus, Dionysus and winemaking, was also sacred to fertility deities as it stood for general abundance, hospitality and having a good time. I especially love to pavé the oak and vine leaves with diamonds.'

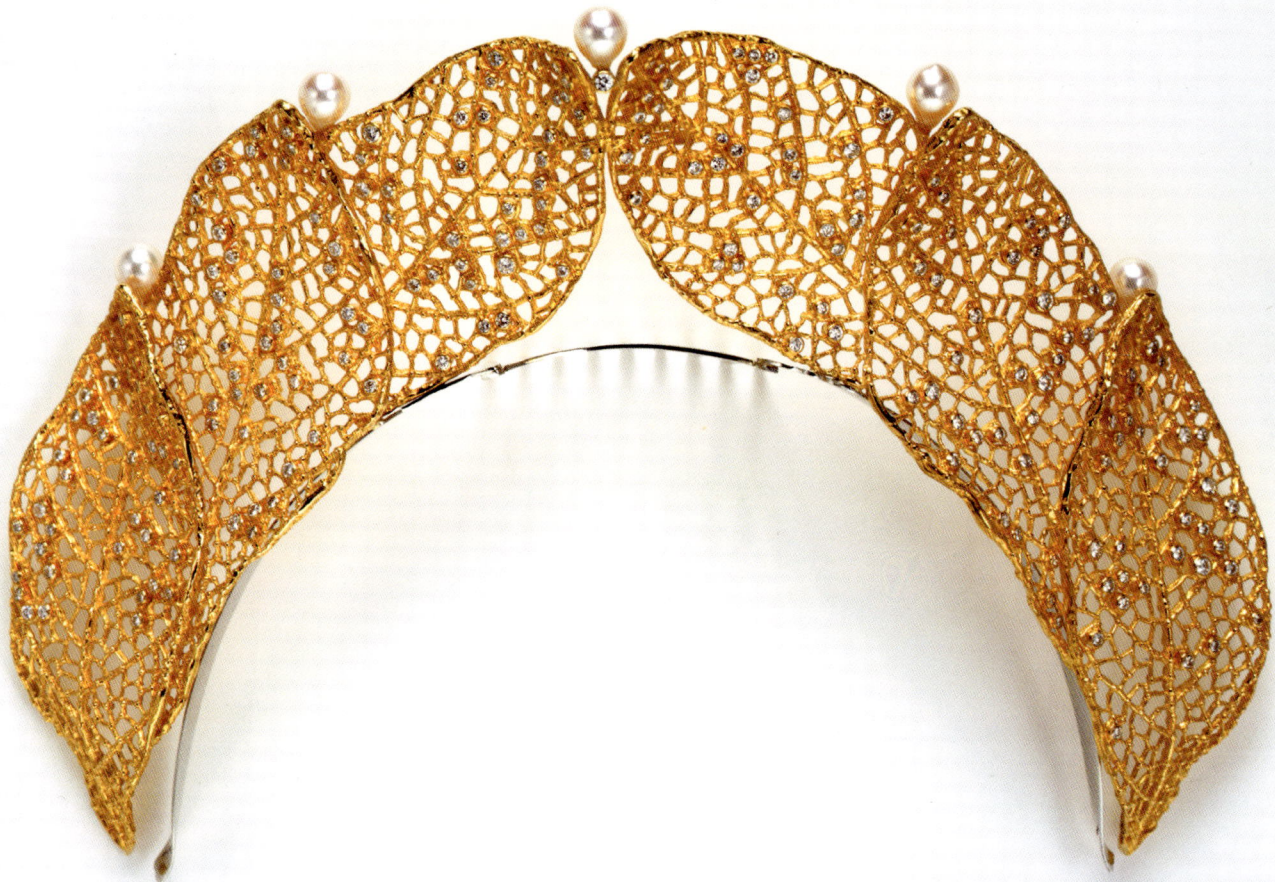

The Anastasia Tiara (2002). Yellow-gold autumn leaves scattered with diamonds and topped with five drop pearls. This piece was especially created for the 2002 V&A 'Tiaras' exhibition. Private collection. [© Elizabeth Gage Ltd]

Opposite: The Anastasia Bracelet (2002). A 22-carat yellow-gold bracelet designed to reflect the shape and form of a fallen autumn leaf. Private collection. [© Elizabeth Gage Ltd]

Flower and Leaf Bangles (2001). Two yellow-gold bangles set with enamel and decorated with hand-engraved leaves and flowers interspersed with brilliant-cut diamonds. Top: Private Collection, Connecticut, USA. Bottom: Private Collection, California, USA. [© Elizabeth Gage Ltd]

Opposite: The Tatiana Pin (1999). A large, oval aquamarine is encircled by white-gold and yellow-gold diamond-set oak leaves and finished with a baroque pearl. Private Collection, Maryland, USA. [© Elizabeth Gage Ltd]

Above: Oak Leaf Pin (1999). Carved and textured yellow-gold oak leaves, signifying strength and friendship, sit atop a glass 19th-century intaglio depicting a party scene. Private Collection, Washington, D.C., USA. [© Elizabeth Gage Ltd]

Below: Vine Leaf Ring (1999). A luminous mandarin garnet surrounded by yellow-gold vine leaves set on a gallery of brown enamel. Elizabeth Gage Archive. [© Elizabeth Gage Ltd]

Opposite: The Palm Leaf Pin (2001). A beautiful, greyish-white South Sea pearl appears from behind a carved yellow-gold leaf atop a diamond-encrusted, nautilus-shaped swirl. Private Collection, New York, USA. Photographed with complementary white-gold oak leaf earrings set with diamonds and accented yellow-gold leaf veins. Private Collection, Massachusetts USA. [© Elizabeth Gage Ltd]

The Autumn Leaves Pin and Matching
Earrings (1998). The pin features a beautiful,
subtle, pinkish-brown fancy-cut tourmaline.
Both the pin and matching earrings are
decorated with yellow-gold leaves and
diamonds on a white-gold background. Pin:
Elizabeth Gage Archive. Earrings: Private
Collection, Florida, USA.
[© Elizabeth Gage Ltd]

Opposite: The Thaina Pin and Matching
Earrings (2002). The set was a commission
based around the emerald-cut aquamarine
and two oval aquamarines owned by the
client. The stones have been framed in
opalescent white enamel decorated with
yellow-gold leaves and diamonds. The pin
is finished with a silver-grey baroque pearl.
Private Collection, Kuwait.
[© Elizabeth Gage Ltd]

The Green Man of the Grape (2006). A carved rock crystal intaglio is set inside a yellow-gold frame decorated with diamond-set flower motifs, carved gold grapes and leaves and eau-de-nil enamel. Elizabeth Gage Archive. [© Elizabeth Gage Ltd]

Opposite: The Green Man Necklace (2001). The head of the Green Man is carved in yellow gold and set on a tiger's eye disc. The pendant hangs from a necklace of tiger's eye beads via a gold funnel decorated with a leaf pattern. Private Collection, Cheshire, UK. [© Elizabeth Gage Ltd]

The Green Man

'Whilst out walking and thinking about a dear female friend of mine who had recently passed away, I clearly heard the words "look after the Green Man". This puzzled me, so I wrote to her husband to ask if the Green Man meant anything to him. It did not. However, months later, I remembered that he had actually served in the Royal Green Jackets (a British infantry regiment). Reflecting upon this, I presumed *he* was the Green Man. When I told him, he laughed and said it was so like his wife, she always said he'd never be able to organise his life without her.

'That was that, or so I thought. Some time later, I was driving to London and listening to the radio, when the presenter announced a forthcoming programme about the Green Man. Intrigued, I went to the library and found two books on him. I devoured them. Haven't you experienced, as I did, having heard something for the first time, that suddenly it was all around you; a heightened awareness? I now notice the Green Man everywhere.

'When I visited a sculptress, I found she was carving a 7-foot Green Man as a commission. A van appeared out of nowhere with 'Green Man Deliveries' in large letters on the side. There were many others. The Green Man even showed his face in Albemarle Street, near my London shop: carved in all his glory, he graced No. 23 in art nouveau style. Not a typical Green Man but one nonetheless.

'The Green Man is composed of leaves, symbolising the union of humanity with the world of vegetation. Originally a pagan symbol, he was integrated into Christian churches and is now a powerful image of fertility, denoting the male energy that impregnates the earth but is still part of the eternal cycle of birth, decay and rebirth.

'To me the Green Man symbolises how important nature is to man, just as man is to nature. One could not live without the other, so it is essential that one does not destroy the other. It seems totally natural, therefore, to incorporate nature into my jewels. I do so in many ways, using leaves and flowers hand-carved in gold with exquisite vibrant enamelling, as well as intaglios carved with a variety of trees. I am thrilled with this new aspect of my work and am happy that my clients love it too.'

The Green Tree Bracelet (1998). Yellow-gold bracelet set with green tourmaline cabochons engraved with five different species of tree. Private Collection, Illinois, USA. [© Elizabeth Gage Ltd]

Opposite: The Green Goddess Necklace (2001). Graduated cabochon peridots framed in repoussé yellow gold and linked with textured gold circles. The stone in the detachable pendant is engraved with a woman looking through a forest. Elizabeth Gage Archive. [© Elizabeth Gage Ltd]

Carved and Coloured Stones

Many of Elizabeth Gage's raw materials are sourced from specialist manufacturer and wholesaler Gustav Caesar in Idar-Oberstein, the world capital of coloured gemstones, located in south-west Germany. Originally a mining town until its agate and jasper deposits were exhausted, it evolved to become an important gemstone centre in the 19th century when emigrants from the town discovered the world's most important agate deposit in Brazil's state of Rio Grande do Sul. Idar-Oberstein went on to become a leading hub in the trade of coloured gemstones from Brazil and Africa and is also known for its local artists who have developed an expertise for carving and engraving precious and semi-precious stones.

Paul-Otto Caesar, fifth-generation managing director of Gustav Caesar, has on numerous occasions hosted Elizabeth Gage at his home in Kirschweiler, and counts himself as a close family friend.

Paul-Otto's first project for Elizabeth Gage was a carving of 'The Head of Janus' in chalcedony from a mine in Namibia renowned for producing the finest blue stones. Janus was the Roman god of new beginnings, which is why they gave his name to the month of January. His image was always depicted with two faces: a youth looking forwards and a bearded older man looking backwards towards the past. He was also the god who presided over conflict; in Rome, the gates to the front and rear of buildings bearing his name were kept open during times of war and closed to mark the arrival of peace. Chalcedony, a stone believed to absorb negative energy and to promote brotherhood and goodwill, was a perfect material for the project.

Since that first collaboration nearly 40 years ago, Paul-Otto Caesar has been a constant presence in the Elizabeth Gage story, and more recently, in November 2023, he organised a party for her at his London club, The Travellers, to celebrate her 60th anniversary as a jewellery designer. 'I think whenever we meet or talk on the phone, the spirit of Janus is still around us.'

Gemstone carver Hans-Ulrich Pauly is another invaluable resource for Elizabeth Gage in Idar-Oberstein. For many years he has been the go-to man whenever she needs a specially carved centrepiece for one of her jewels. Pauly is descended from a long line of master lapidaries; his art ranges from contemporary cameos and portrait carvings to three-dimensional sculptures. His work is widely admired for its exacting detail and his ability to capture a subject and bring it to life.

The following pieces serve to illustrate the artistic and lapidary skills of the stone cutters, carvers and engravers of Idar-Oberstein.

Opposite: Green Tourmaline and Pearl Necklace (1988). Three rows of cultured pink pearls terminating in diamond-set hook-end fittings. The pendant features a central faceted, oval green tourmaline framed with gold set with faceted, round sapphires and diamonds, with diamond-set carved gold plinths at each quarter. Photographed with complementary earrings and ring. Private collection. [© Elizabeth Gage Ltd]

Valois Earrings and Templar Ring (1997). An oval rubellite cabochon centres on an opaque brown-and-white enamel patterned background. The earrings are topped by carved diamond plinths and feature cultured pearls in polished caps at the bottom. The wide tapered ring features gold wire detailing on the shank and diamond detailing to the collet of the rubellite setting. Private collection, Saudi Arabia. [© Elizabeth Gage Ltd]

Opposite: The Cleopatra Necklace (1990). Fourteen aquamarine crystals alternating with granulated yellow-gold sections to complete the circle. Private Collection, Florida, USA. [© Elizabeth Gage Ltd]

This page, clockwise from top left:
Garnet Ring (2000). A chequerboard-cut rhodolite garnet encircled by a black-and-white opaque enamel pattern. The black enamel pattern continues on the sides of ring. Private collection, Massachusetts, USA. [© Elizabeth Gage Ltd]

The Strawberry Hill Gothic Ring (1994). A large faceted, oval rubellite tourmaline set in ornately carved yellow gold and decorated with pavé-set diamonds. Private collection, New York, USA. [© Elizabeth Gage Ltd]

God of Wind Pendant (1998). A carved labradorite cameo with gold 'ruffle' collar, set above a large, 119-carat aquamarine crystal. Private collection, Illinois, USA. [© Elizabeth Gage Ltd]

Opposite: The Blue Water Necklace (1991). Ten beautifully cut aquamarines set simply in yellow gold and linked together with gold loops. Photographed with complementary ring and earrings. Private Collection, Tennessee, USA. [© Elizabeth Gage Ltd]

Tourmaline and Aquamarine Pin (1972). Three cabochon aquamarines and two tourmalines set in yellow gold and decorated with pearls and rubies. V&A, London. [© Elizabeth Gage Ltd]

'Sputnik' Earrings (1971). Pearls and diamonds set in contrasting polished and matte yellow gold. Elizabeth Gage Archive. [© Elizabeth Gage Ltd]

Opposite: The Celeste Pin and Earrings (1989). Rare indicolite tourmalines set in yellow gold and elaborately decorated with South Sea pearls, rubies and diamonds. Private Collection, Washington, D.C., USA. [© Elizabeth Gage Ltd]

The Sunrise Pin (1993). A 'Sun-Man' face carved from citrine is set in granulated yellow gold studded with coloured and white diamonds. The back of the citrine is shaped to throw light through the stone and the gold work designed to represent the sun's flashing rays. Private collection, Washington, USA. [© Elizabeth Gage Ltd]

Opposite: Amethyst Pendant (1981). Two rows of amethyst beads alternately linked by granulated yellow gold plaques decorated with gold wire and granulated gold rondels. The pendant comprises a large, oval 'Rose de France' amethyst set inside a bombé granulated gold frame, pavé-set with faceted round amethysts. Private collection, UK. [© Elizabeth Gage Ltd]

Kiss Pin (1988). Faceted pink tourmalines set in yellow gold with cultured grey pearls in wire funnels to the diagonals. The outer stones are topped with diamonds set in white gold carved plinths. The centre stone has a white gold and pavé-set diamond surround. Suspended from the base is a triangular green tourmaline cabochon. Photographed with matching Valois earrings. Private collection, New York, USA. [© Elizabeth Gage Ltd]

Opposite: The Renaissance Necklace (1988). This classically shaped pendant features a vivid blue pear-shaped tourmaline set in yellow gold and decorated with pearls and rubies. It hangs from a yellow-gold link necklace. Elizabeth Gage Archive. [© Elizabeth Gage Ltd]

This page, clockwise from top left:

Templar Ring (2009). A bi-coloured, sugar-loaf cabochon tourmaline set in yellow gold; the wide shank is tapered and decorated with black enamel chevron patterns to the sides. Elizabeth Gage Archive. [© Elizabeth Gage Ltd]

The Solar Prince Pin (1988). A carved opal depicting Horus with his wings outstretched, set in yellow gold, and his head encircled with a granulated yellow-gold 'sun halo' topped with a diamond set in a yellow-gold plinth. A large cabochon emerald at the base reflects the colours of the opal. The wings represent a true talisman of the Egyptian God, Horus. Elizabeth Gage Archive. [© Elizabeth Gage Ltd]

Knight with Falcon Pin (1996). An extraordinary carved yellow beryl shows a knight with a falcon on his arm, riding through an archway depicting a mythical creature. The piece, which is set in yellow gold and topped with an oval blue topaz, features a crystal aquamarine in its natural form at its base. Private Collection, Indiana, USA. [© Elizabeth Gage Ltd]

Opposite: The 'Sienna' Pin (2008). A central labradorite snail shell cameo is set in yellow gold and surrounded by six carved citrine petals. Each petal is decorated with black enamel circles to its back surface. Elizabeth Gage Archive. [© Elizabeth Gage Ltd]

The Renaissance Pendant (1994). A central blue emerald-cut tourmaline set in yellow gold, decorated with white enamel, rubies and prasiolites and a large pearl drop. The Pendant hangs from a pearl and yellow-gold chain. Private collection, Saudi Arabia. [© Elizabeth Gage Ltd]

Opposite: The Serenity Necklace (1992). Perfectly matched and, therefore, very rare luminous blue chalcedony beads and two carved, granulated yellow-gold beads strung with polished gold spacers with beaded gold edgings. Photographed with a complementary blue chalcedony ring. Private collection, Texas, USA. [© Elizabeth Gage Ltd]

CHAPTER 5

Design Philosophy and Legacy

In choosing a vocation, Elizabeth Gage was always likely to pursue some kind of creative endeavour. The artistic gene, inherited through the female line, expressed itself forcefully and this, coupled with the manual dexterity she cultivated at an early age whilst convalescing from a childhood illness, reinforced an innate proclivity.

Indeed, both her siblings were also creative types: her sister, Anne, became a dress designer and opened a shop selling ballgowns in Beauchamp Place, whilst her brother, Robin, became a furniture designer based in Pimlico.

Although born in England, Elizabeth acquired and maintained an international outlook having spent her early childhood in New York and Washington during the war and via family connections to France, where her grandmother and parents spent much of their time. This unparochial perspective, whether wittingly or unwittingly, fed into her approach to business and, in particular, to the idea that it was quite natural to develop a client base on both sides of the Atlantic.

Her innate abilities were formally honed at the Chelsea School of Art in the 1950s and complemented by the craft skills in silver and goldsmithing she acquired at the Sir John Cass College in the 1960s. From here she emerged almost fully formed and the early pieces she made were eagerly purchased by clients who recognised that here was someone capable of creating new, exciting forms unavailable elsewhere in London.

Her precocious talent was instantly recognised by Cartier in New York, resulting in a major commission. This convinced her she was on the right path and, furthermore, that it made business sense to focus on designing rather than making. Commercial success soon followed.

The immediate post-war landscape for jewellery had undergone a period of stagnation, partly caused by austerity and very high taxation on luxury goods. As a consequence, much of what was being purchased at the time was second-hand or else inexpensive and aesthetically uninteresting.

Old money kept its diamond parures in the safe waiting to be dusted down for formal occasions; the bourgeoisie contented itself with star and crescent brooches, flower sprays, and the little cats, dogs and horseshoes to be seen in the windows of jewellery shops up and down the country; and the new money didn't really arrive until the Swinging Sixties.

The austerity of the 1950s eventually receded and gave way to an age of optimism and affluence. For the jewellery industry, this was manifested by the groundbreaking International Exhibition of Modern Jewellery 1890–1961 organised by the Goldsmiths' Company in association with the V&A. The exhibition, which ran from 26 October to 2 December 1961 at Goldsmiths' Hall, heralded a new era of modernist jewellery design

Previous page: Elizabeth Gage and Bertie at 5 West Halkin Street, London SW1, in 2019. [© Mark Langridge]

Moonstone Ring. A model based on the original drawing is carved in wax and then cast in gold. Here, the goldsmith files the inside of the shank before setting the main stone. [© Elizabeth Gage Ltd]

fronted by London-based independent jewellers such as Andrew Grima, John Donald, David Thomas, Gerda Flöckinger and Charles de Temple.

By the time Elizabeth Gage started out as a jeweller in the mid-1960s, this modern aesthetic, characterised by textured gold and abstracted organic forms, was firmly established and well on the way to becoming an international movement. In doing so it had helped to foster London's reputation as a global creative hub for jewellery design alongside music, fashion, film and any other cultural pursuit one could care to mention. In short, it was a trend that had been done and done well but Elizabeth's artistic inclinations lay elsewhere.

As recounted in an earlier chapter, the genesis of her interest in jewellery...or 'epiphany' as she describes it, originated in the British Museum in the form of a display cabinet replete with ancient, hammered gold rings. This was the first time she had encountered jewellery she actually wanted to possess and to wear. In that moment, the disparate elements of her character – the love of history, the creative impulse, the ability to corral her imagination into design forms and craft them into real objects – all came together as a whole. She had finally discovered something she could do with her life that was absorbing, challenging and realistically achievable. All she had to do now was learn how to make jewellery!

Elizabeth Gage's great gift is her ability to fuse ancient and modern influences into a style that is very much her own. She is fascinated by the characters and events portrayed in history. Indeed, her first historical hero, The Count of St Germain, was closely affiliated with the mystical societies of the day such as the Freemasons, Illuminati, Rosicrucians and Templars. He was acquainted with practically everyone worth knowing in the 18th century, including King Louis XV of France, Madame de Pompadour, Marie Antoinette and Catherine the Great. Furthermore, he appears to have been a pioneering alchemist who claimed to be capable of transforming base metal into an alloy resembling gold, removing flaws from diamonds and enhancing the colour and lustre of coloured gemstones through heat treatment.

Alongside her fascination for historical characters, Elizabeth is an obsessive collector of coins, cameos and historic artefacts; a lover of nature in all its forms; and is intrigued by the hidden symbolism contained in art, poetry and literature over the centuries. These natural interests, inclinations and preferences are constantly referenced in her work and woven into the creative process.

The names she gives to jewels – Agincourt, Templar, Charlemagne, Valois... – evoke history, chivalry and pageantry. Her design style, choice of stones, use of materials and way of making also reference the aesthetic of those times. However, there is always another, stronger element present in her jewellery that is pure Elizabeth Gage. What this is exactly, is hard to put into words, it is a kind of alchemy, but you know it when you see it.

Her natural temperament is that of an optimist and risk-taker. She does not appear to be someone who frets or is consumed with self-doubt. On the contrary, she displays the confidence of someone who has always followed her instincts and more often than not they have proven to be justified. Of course, this type of attitude has to be backed up by talent, energy, even a dash of luck and this has certainly been the case with Elizabeth.

Her bold designs and vision have always attracted strong-willed, empowered women who have cultivated their own personal style and are more than capable of making their own decisions when it comes to choosing jewellery and, indeed, to paying for it themselves. Elizabeth's designs since coming to market have always been synonymous with individuality and timeless style and, as such, have become a staple for any jewellery connoisseur's collection.

Another quality appreciated by women is the fact that Elizabeth Gage jewellery is designed to be versatile and practical. From the get-go, she was determined to design pieces that could be worn 'day into night', hence a preference for yellow gold to catch the sunlight juxtaposed with bold, colourful, gemstones suited to refract moonlight and candlelight. Another aspect of her approach is that her jewels are comfortable to wear with smooth, tapered or articulated shanks and bezels and without claws or sharp edges, so as not to catch on clothing.

Elizabeth is somewhat reticent when asked about her design process: 'I don't want to give all my secrets away!' The obvious answer would be 'if only it were that simple', but this much she is prepared to concede: it always starts with a stone or central object such as a carving, artefact or fossil. This is followed by a pencil drawing accompanied by the assembly of secondary materials (complementary stones, pearls, small diamonds etc.) plus descriptions and annotations.

This is also the point where Elizabeth's imagination kicks in. More often than not there is an element of storytelling, historical context, mythology and personification involved. Which era is to be evoked? How would the jewel have been worn, and in which setting? Who or what is depicted in the coin or artefact and what is their story? If the carved centrepiece is a bird, an animal or mythical creature – what is its name? Is it male or female? Which symbolic references and associations could be integrated into the design to support the theme? This is where the real magic happens.

Now that the design has been conceived and drafted, a discussion with her craftsmen and production manager can take place. This stage is facilitated by the many years they have experienced working with Elizabeth and, consequently, there is an intuition and understanding about what she wants to achieve.

Each Elizabeth Gage jewel is entirely handmade in England. For many years all the making took place in West Halkin Street but as her craftsmen began moving out of the city, it

Tapered Templar Ring set with emeralds and diamonds. Adding the finishing touches to the original painted design. [© Elizabeth Gage Ltd]

Opposite: Tapered Templar Ring. Cast gold ring prior to setting.
[© Elizabeth Gage Ltd]

became apparent that too much working time was being wasted commuting back and forth. Today, production is overseen by Andrew Behennah, a Cornishman who has worked with Elizabeth Gage for over 30 years. Andrew works in the West Halkin Street office and two or three times a week sits with Elizabeth to discuss design specifications for new pieces. Her goldsmiths, enamellers, stone setters, polishers and stringers, who now all work remotely, travel up to London whenever required to be briefed by Elizabeth and Andrew.

Elizabeth's head goldsmith for many years was Jim Webb, who ran the workshop when she decided to step away from the bench in order to focus instead on designing. Jim trained and managed a team of four goldsmiths who made for Elizabeth Gage throughout the 1980s and '90s. Phil Barnes (and before him, his father Fred) was Elizabeth's chief enameller from the early 1970s and for the next 50 years. Not only was Phil an award-winning enameller, he was also a brilliant engraver who made pieces under his own name as well as for many of the leading fine jewellery and *objet* houses of the day.

Jim Webb has since retired, and Phil Barnes sadly passed away in 2019. However, the core of the team assembled by Jim remains. Today, Elizabeth Gage jewels continue to be made by the highly experienced goldsmiths Mark Woolley, Kevin Ricks and Gonny van der Vegte, with the addition of enameller Paul Munn. The big advantage of many decades of collaboration between designer and craftsmen is that everyone knows the Elizabeth Gage way of doing things, resulting in a common language and even a kind of telepathy evolving between the various protagonists.

The archive spanning Elizabeth Gage's 60-year career contains over 30,000 individual designs. Maintaining this level of quality, at volume, year in year out is a phenomenal achievement for a single creative mind. The big houses cannot and do not work in this way; the majority of their designs are computer aided and manufactured in the Far East. This is the reality of 'mass' as opposed to 'genuine' luxury.

Over time, Elizabeth Gage has developed design signatures that are specific to her work, and which characterise her style. The most obvious of these is the fact that many of her designs reference history and, in particular the Age of Antiquity, the Middle Ages and the Renaissance. These were times when the aesthetic was bolder, more symbolic and, in many respects, more in tune with a modern sensibility. Victorian and Edwardian jewellery can often be over-elaborate and fussy, while in much of contemporary fine jewellery, the personality of the designer is invisible, resulting in pieces that are sometimes rather bland and formulaic.

Feeding into Elizabeth's love of history is a passion for collecting coins and historical artefacts from auctions, markets and dealers. They never stay in her possession too long, however, as she cannot resist incorporating them into her jewels.

References to nature, animals and sea creatures also feature prominently in her work. These are things she loves not only for their life force and beauty but also for their symbolism and special meaning in Christian and pagan mythology throughout the ages and across the world. Some are sculpted to order in Idar-Oberstein, others repurposed from ancient bronze relics. Whatever the origin, to Elizabeth, each flower or leaf has a meaning and a narrative, each creature a name and a character.

Motifs with symbolic connotations also feature in Elizabeth Gage's designs, typically as secondary or supporting elements: myrtle leaves stand for love, beauty and loyalty; vine leaves for growth and regeneration; oak leaves for power and victory; roses for love and passion; the sun stands for clarity, energy and positivity; whilst the moon signals change and uncertainty. Elizabeth uses these and many other symbols and motifs in her work and each conveys a specific sentiment and meaning.

Other elements deployed by Elizabeth are purely decorative: enamelwork is used to add colour and contrast; gold is twisted, hammered, granulated, carved and engraved to give texture and add detail; and small diamonds are deployed as accents to catch the light. The many signature techniques used to make Elizabeth Gage jewellery are closely guarded secrets to the extent that in some instances, she will not even share them with her goldsmiths, preferring instead to 'disappear behind the curtain' to perform her alchemy.

The final important characteristic of Elizabeth Gage's work is her use of yellow gold, semi-precious stones and other unconventional materials, such as fossils and polished hardstones preferred for their limitless array of colours and their intrinsic beauty rather than mere intrinsic value. The use of such materials was uncommon when Elizabeth began her career in the 1960s, as the convention in those days was to use a limited palette of diamonds, sapphires, emeralds, rubies, pearls and, perhaps, the odd aquamarine set in platinum.

The title of Elizabeth's first monograph *The Unconventional Gage* sums up perfectly her design philosophy and attitude to making jewellery. In choosing a path, she rejected both the prevailing norms of her industry and the modernist revolution about to set the scene for the next 20 years. Instead, she chose to incorporate elements of the distant past into her work in a way that was simultaneously inventive and modern. In doing so, she created a style that was bold, enigmatic and instantly recognisable as Elizabeth Gage. Her enduring success is testament to the fact that her clients understand and value these traits.

The list of internationally renowned post-war jewellery designers is short. The number of women on this list is shorter still: Elsa Peretti, Marina B, Wendy Ramshaw, Barbara Cartlidge, Gerda Flöckinger and Vivianna Torun Bülow-Hübe are the few that spring to mind, but it would not be complete without adding the name Elizabeth Gage.

Shiraz Pin. Setting the intaglio, diamonds and pearl drop to create the finished piece. [© Elizabeth Gage Ltd]

Opposite: Shiraz Pin. Positioning a glass intaglio and marquise diamonds on a wax model according to the original painted design. [© Elizabeth Gage Ltd]

Painted Designs

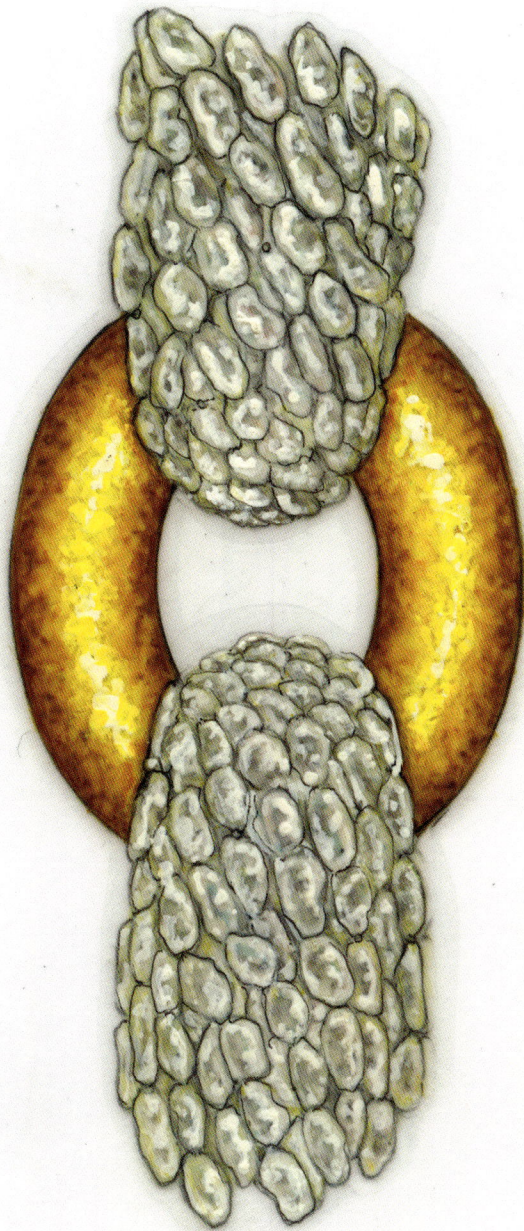

The following pages contain a selection of hand-painted gouache watercolour designs. These are based on Elizabeth's own annotated pencil drawings, which – after consultation with her production manager, Andrew Behennah – are sent to the art department to be formally worked into colour illustrations of what the finished pieces will look like.

These painted designs, drawn to scale, are used by her goldsmiths as references during the manufacturing process. They are also shown to clients before a bespoke piece of jewellery is commissioned and made. There are many hundreds of such paintings in the Elizabeth Gage Archive and each of them can undoubtedly be considered as a work of art in its own right.

Previous page: Necklace design (1996). Multiple rows of freshwater pearls loop through a bombé oval repoussé yellow-gold fitting. [© Elizabeth Gage Ltd]

Opposite: Ring design (1998). Yellow-gold and black-enamel set with a faceted yellow sapphire and diamonds. [© Elizabeth Gage Ltd]

Ring design (1999). Yellow gold set with a large round diamond. The gallery is decorated with brown enamel and a gold vine leaf pattern. [© Elizabeth Gage Ltd]

Opposite: Charlemagne Ring design (1992). Yellow-gold set with an oval amethyst intaglio, rubies and diamonds, and decorated with purple enamel. [© Elizabeth Gage Ltd]

B

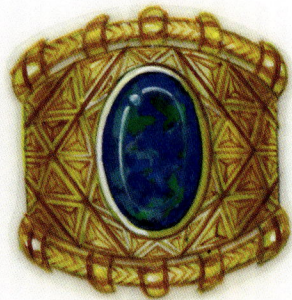

Agincourt Ring design (1991). Yellow gold set with an oval black opal.
[© Elizabeth Gage Ltd]

Opposite: Pisces Zodiac Ring design (1997). Yellow and white gold.
[© Elizabeth Gage Ltd]

Templar Ring design (1999). Yellow gold, set with an oval carnelian cabochon and decorated with red enamel chevrons. [© Elizabeth Gage Ltd]

Opposite: Sun Ring design (1993). Yellow gold, set with a round mabé pearl and diamonds. [© Elizabeth Gage Ltd]

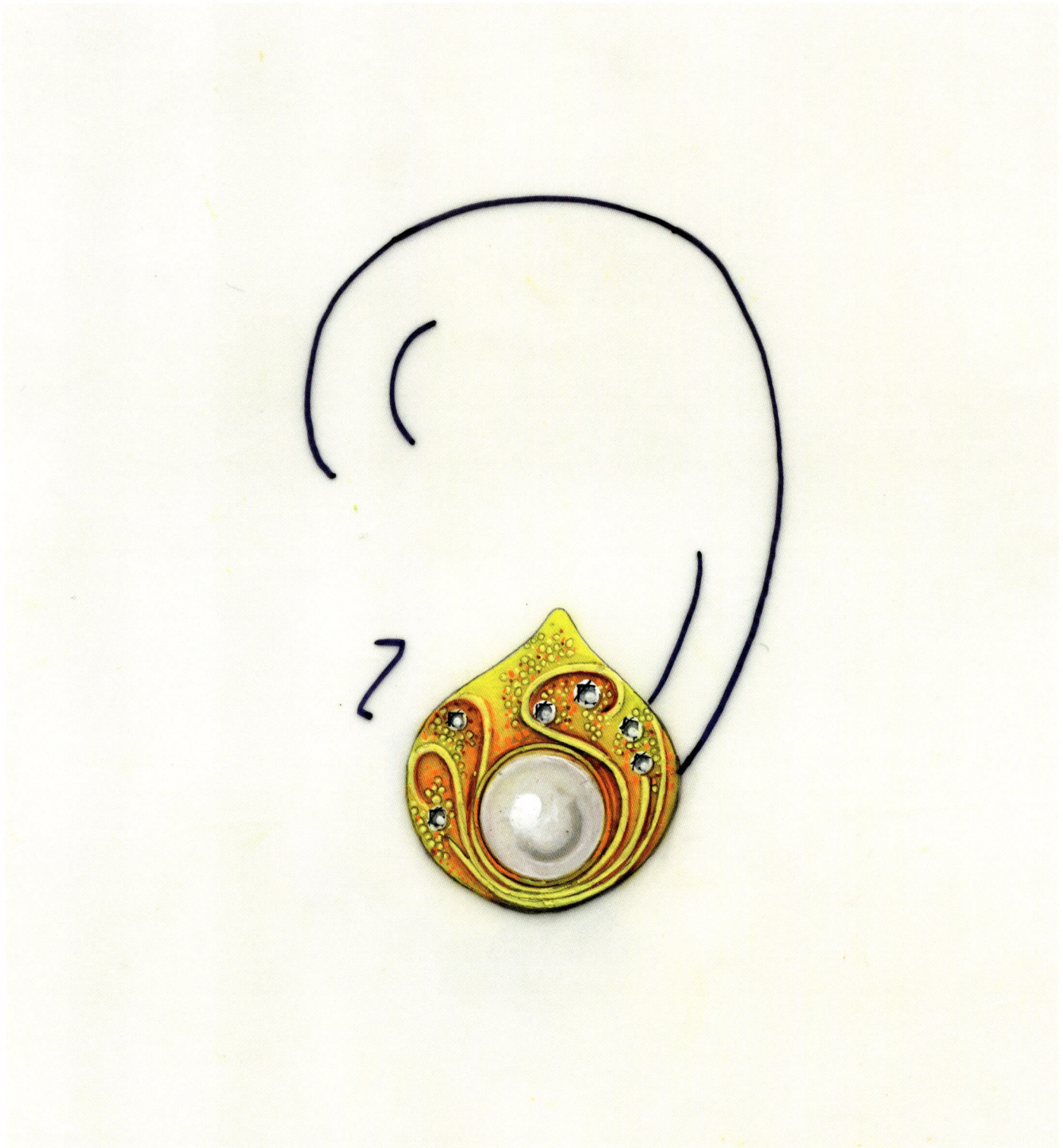

Shiraz Earring design (1994). Yellow gold with wire and granulation
embellishment, set with a Mabé pearl and diamonds. [@ Elizabeth Gage Ltd]

Opposite: Lion Earring design (1997). A citrine cameo lion set in orange
enamel decorated with yellow-gold myrtle leaves. [@ Elizabeth Gage Ltd]

Bombé Earring design (1991). Yellow gold with wire and granulation embellishment, pavé-set with diamonds. [© Elizabeth Gage Ltd]

Opposite: Black Panther Earring design (1991). Carved onyx panthers with coral tongues and white agate teeth, set in repoussé yellow-gold spirals decorated with black enamel clubs. [© Elizabeth Gage Ltd]

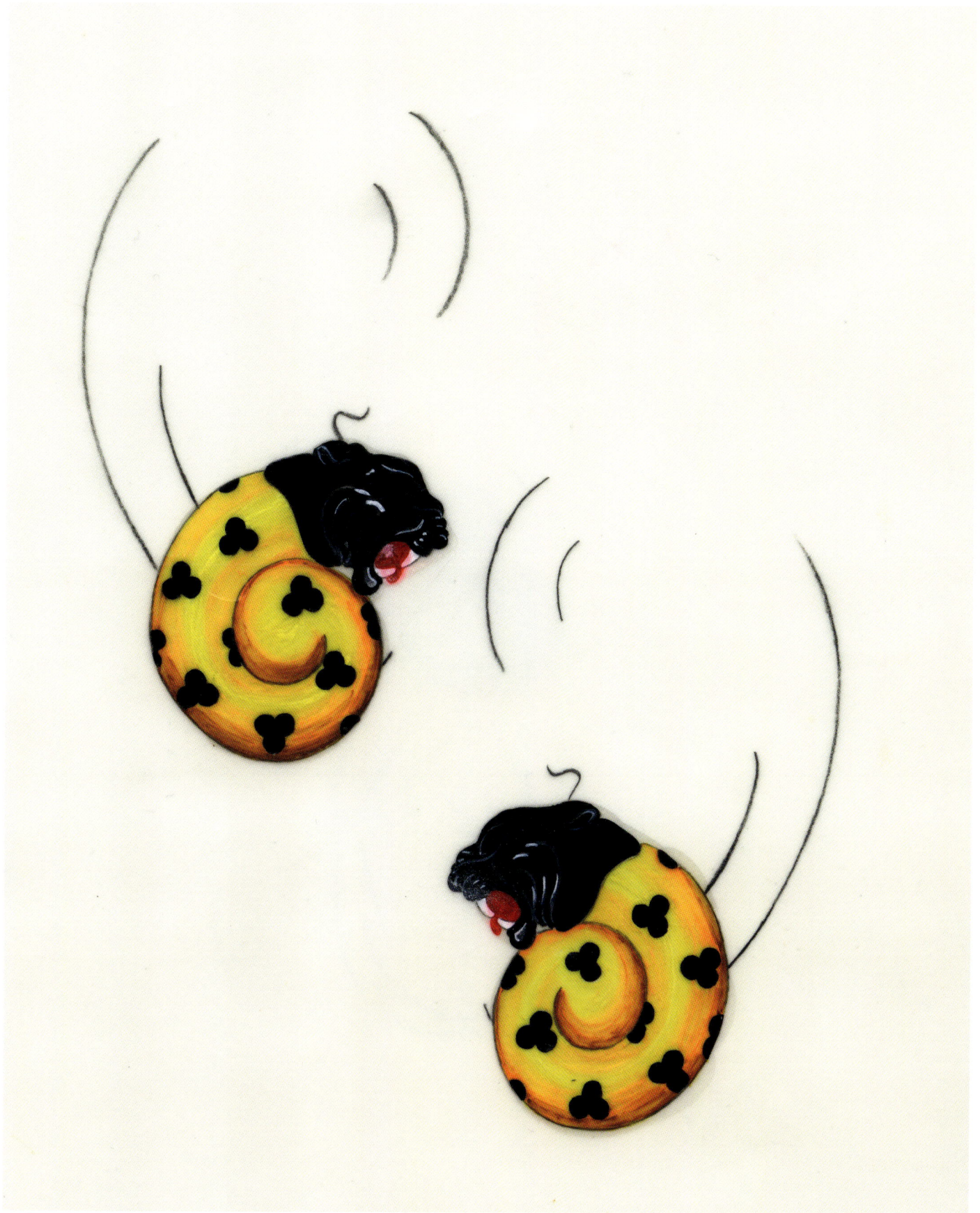

African Queen Earring design (1990). A large, oval mabé pearl set in a yellow-gold twisted wire frame topped with a diamond-set plinth with three carnelian beads in wire funnels at the base. [© Elizabeth Gage Ltd]

Opposite: African Queen Earring design (1990). Yellow gold set with a central oval cabochon agate framed in red enamel, with two onyx beads at the base and plume pearl to the top. [© Elizabeth Gage Ltd]

Acanthus Leaf Pin design (1994). Granulated, repoussé yellow-gold set with diamonds and pearls. [© Elizabeth Gage Ltd]

Opposite, top: Shiraz Pin design (1989). Yellow gold set with two oval sapphires and diamonds, and wire and granulation embellishment. [© Elizabeth Gage Ltd]

Opposite, bottom: Elizabeth I Pin design (1995). The centrepiece is a silver Elizabeth I coin set inside a yellow-gold and red enamel frame, topped with a diamond-set plinth. The lower yellow-gold frame is set with a cabochon jasper engraved with a Tudor rose motif. The two circular frames are separated by two cultured pearls in wire funnels. [© Elizabeth Gage Ltd]

Kiss Pin design (1990s). An oval obsidian 'Phoenix' intaglio framed in yellow gold and surrounded by alternating oval mabé pearls set in yellow-gold frames and grey pearls held in gold scalloped funnels with red enamel highlights. [© Elizabeth Gage Ltd]

Opposite: Leopard's Head Pin design (1997). A petrified palm leopard's head set above a round, bombé red enamel body decorated with yellow-gold myrtle leaves. [© Elizabeth Gage Ltd]

Kiss Pin design (1998). An oval red jasper cameo set in yellow gold, surrounded by alternating oval mabé pearls in yellow-gold frames topped with diamond-set plinths and grey pearls held in yellow-gold wire funnels. [© Elizabeth Gage Ltd]

Opposite: Parrot's Head Pin design (2004). A carved tsavorite parrot's head with Tahitian pearl beak and painted rock crystal eye set inside two engraved yellow-gold feathers separated by an oval green beryl. [© Elizabeth Gage Ltd]

Bamboo Cane Bangle design (1980s). Coral decorated with yellow-gold bands set with diamonds. [© Elizabeth Gage Ltd]

Opposite: White Bangle design (1986). A linen-textured white-gold bangle embellished with yellow-gold wires, yellow-gold beads, and set with rubies and diamonds. [© Elizabeth Gage Ltd]

Articulated Agincourt Bracelet design (1989). Yellow gold set with diamonds and rubies. [© Elizabeth Gage Ltd]

Opposite: Articulated Agincourt Bracelet design (1989). Yellow gold decorated with gold beads and diamonds. [© Elizabeth Gage Ltd]

a.

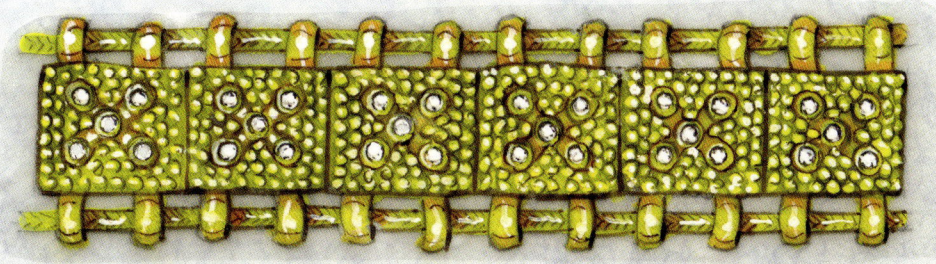

b.

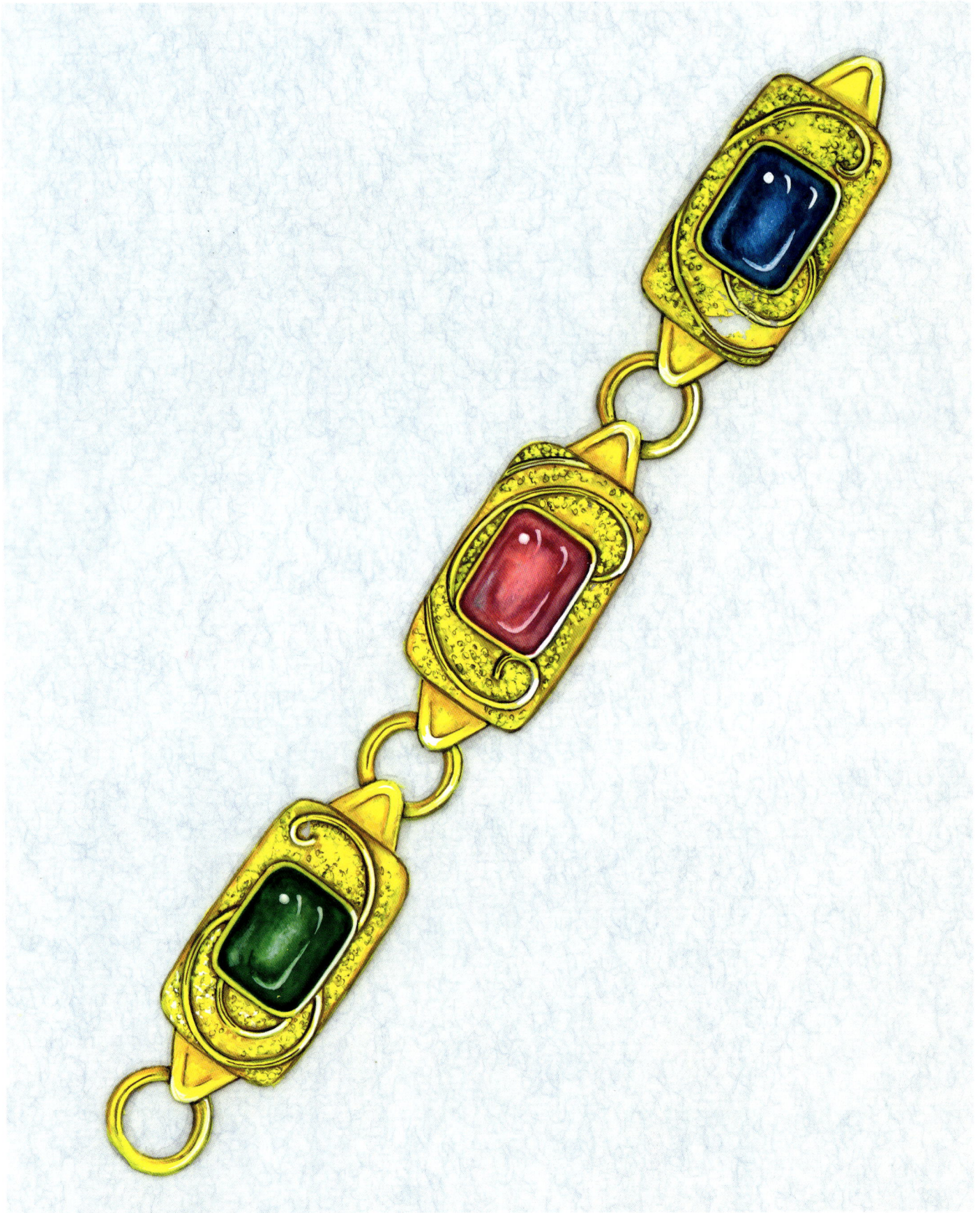

Ebony Bangle design (1980s). Polished ebony decorated with molten yellow-gold bands and diamonds. [© Elizabeth Gage Ltd]

Opposite: Gold Link Bracelet design (1990). Yellow-gold plaques embellished with gold wire and granulation, set with rectangular cabochon sapphire, red tourmaline and green tourmaline, connected by circular yellow-gold links. [© Elizabeth Gage Ltd]

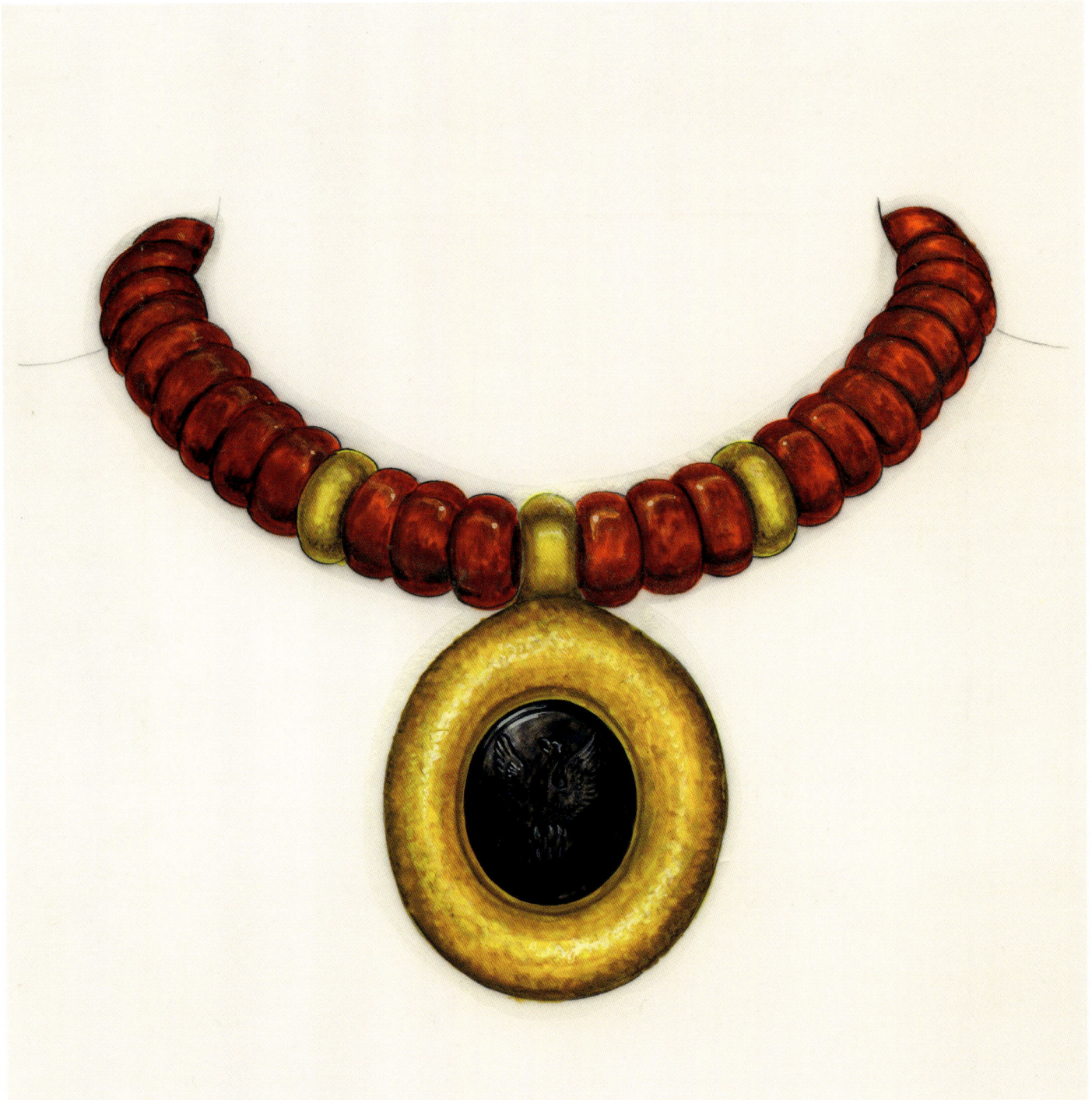

Phoenix Pendant design (1993). An oval obsidian 'Phoenix' intaglio framed in repoussé yellow gold suspended from a carnelian and gold bead necklace. [© Elizabeth Gage Ltd]

Opposite: Ebony Choker design (1980s). Polished ebony edged with yellow gold and studded with gold beads separated by turquoise spacer discs. Matching earring design: turquoise discs in yellow gold with a polished ebony bead to the base. [© Elizabeth Gage Ltd]

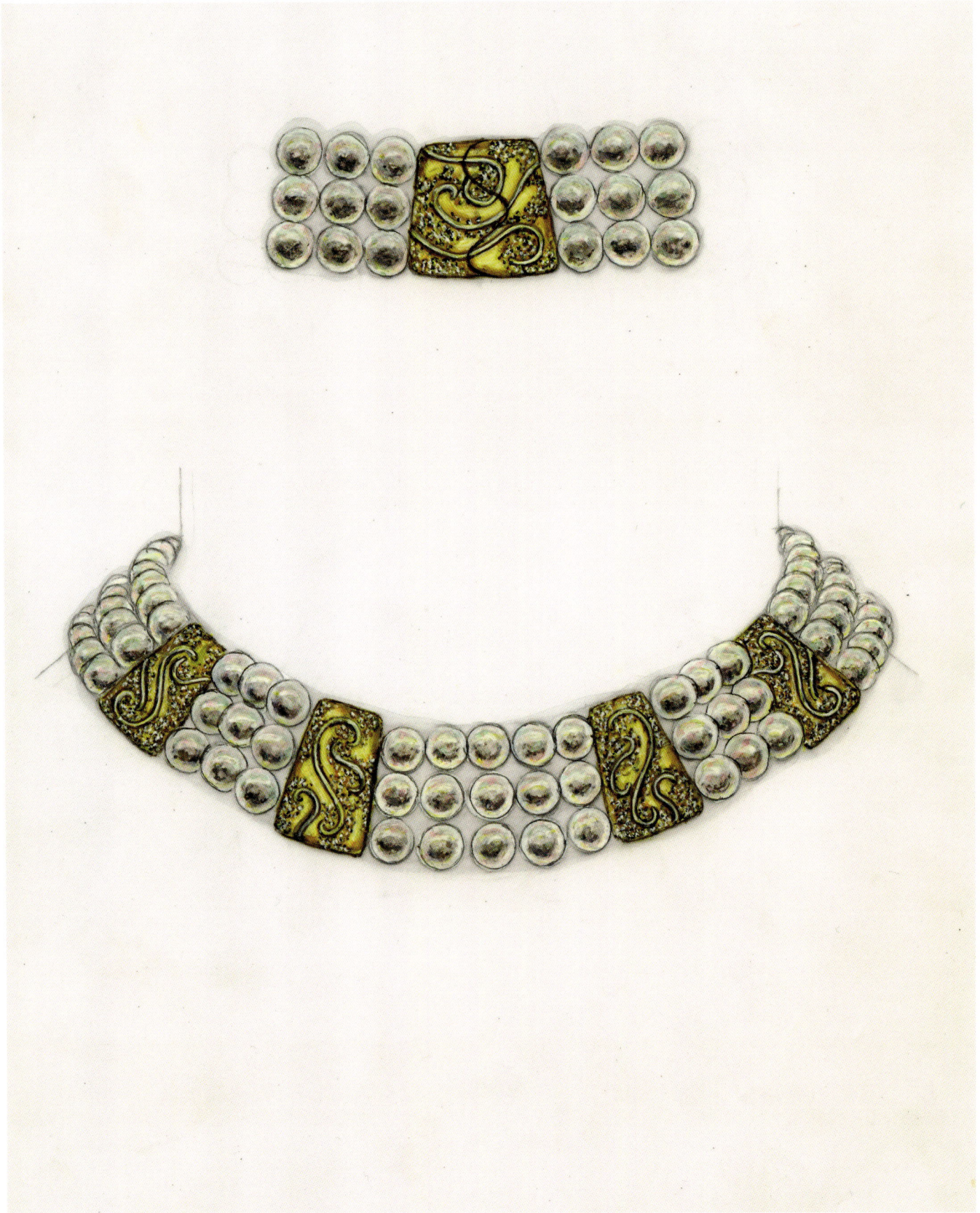

Unicorn Pendant and Pearl Necklace design. A carved black tourmaline cameo with a hammered gold surround set with rubies. The pendant is suspended from a freshwater pearl necklace ending with ruby-set yellow-gold funnel details. [@ Elizabeth Gage Ltd]

Opposite: Pearl Necklace design (1989). Three rows of white cultured pearls strung between yellow-gold plaques and clasp embellished with wire and granulation. [@ Elizabeth Gage Ltd]

Acknowledgements

I am grateful to Elizabeth Gage for inviting me to write her story. Collaborating with her on this project has been a distinctly pleasurable experience. I have thoroughly enjoyed our weekly conversations at her home in Belgravia, sitting under the inquisitive gaze of her beloved Shih Tzu, Bertie. I feel we have since become firm friends – and from the dog, a level of forbearance has been attained, if not genuine warmth.

It is clear to me, having encountered many people who know her in the course of writing this monograph, that Elizabeth Gage is held in huge affection, and rightly so. She wears her accomplishments lightly, but deserves the accolades the jewellery industry has bestowed upon her and the respect and admiration of her peers.

I would also like to thank all those who contributed to the realisation of this book, and in particular:

Joanne Rees, Managing Director of Elizabeth Gage Limited, who engaged me to write Elizabeth's biography. Jo has been a true godsend and a consistent source of encouragement and guidance.

Andrew Behennah, who has brought to light the operational and technical side of the business and assiduously checked and edited the captions.

Nelly Hill, Elizabeth's devoted PA, who behind the scenes has organised, corralled and chivvied in such a way as to make my task that much easier.

Our publisher, James Smith, and his team at ACC, in particular, our editor Susannah Hecht, and the designers Mariona Vilarós Capella and Craig Holden. It has once again been a pleasure to work with them, and we are delighted with the result.

And finally, I would like to thank, on Elizabeth's behalf, all those with whom she has collaborated and from whom she has received support over the span of her career. Without them, nothing could have been achieved.

Front Cover: The Aslan Pin (1994). See page 96. [© Elizabeth Gage Ltd]

Frontispiece: The Sunrise Pin (1993). See page 138. [© Elizabeth Gage Ltd]

ISBN: 978 1 78884 349 2

Editor: Susannah Hecht
Designer: Craig Holden, Mariona Vilarós Capella
Reprographics Manager: Corban Wilkin

EU GPSR Authorised Representative:
Easy Access System Europe Oü, 16879218
Address: Mustamäe tee 50, 10621 Tallinn, Estonia
Email: gpsr@easproject.com Tel: +358 40 500 3575

FSC
www.fsc.org
MIX
Paper | Supporting responsible forestry
FSC® C105997

Printed in Slovenia by Green Leaf Production
for ACC Art Books Ltd, Woodbridge, Suffolk, UK

www.accartbooks.com

ACC
ART
BOOKS